asian
tapas

small bites, big flavors

Christophe Megel and Anton Kilayko

foreword by
Alain Ducasse

introduction by
Judy Sarris and Leanne Kitchen

photography by
Edmond Ho

styling by
Christina Ong and Magdalene Ong

PERIPLUS

contents

the essence of contemporary cooking

Today's cuisine is a living art reflecting modern lifestyles and ideas. It also reflects today's society—which is experiencing an explosion of cultural diversity. There are so many ways of eating well today, and so many reasons and occasions to celebrate. More than ever, eating is an act of sharing where the conversation, flavors and settings provide a vehicle for exchange. Food, in this context, is a profound source of cultural enrichment and communication.

Contemporary cooking has become a citizen of the world. People learn as they travel and share ideas with one another. Our customers are well informed and compare everything with what they have seen or tasted elsewhere. Modern cooking is therefore a cuisine of liberation—where one is free to invent, borrow and create. The old models are obsolete, although basic culinary principles continue to provide a basis for new flavors and sensations.

All of this is by way of saying how happy I am to see a book which so thoroughly embodies the essence and attitude of contemporary cooking. Christophe Megel has traveled the globe, and for him modern cuisine is not an abstract concept. He brings to this project twenty years of experience in France, the United States and now Asia, where he teams up with Anton Kilayko. The recipes in this book illustrate both authors' many-faceted talents. They portray a keen intelligence, a passion for produce, a great imagination and a rigor of method.

I would like to thank them for writing this book. Food enthusiasts will rejoice at the elegance and inventiveness of recipes which virtually anyone can prepare. Above all else, this book invites us to experience many more delicious moments of conviviality—which after all is the true essence of contemporary cooking.

Alain Ducasse

innovative flavors from the new asia

Here is a book that will have you itching to get into the kitchen to chop, slice, mix and blend your way through the imaginative and enthralling ideas contained within its pages, to recreate some of the best new flavors to yet come out of contemporary Asia. Many of the recipes are likely to become favorites—providing quick and delicious everyday snacks and meals—while others offer the challenge and the means to bring new levels of creativity to familiar ingredients and ideas. In a nutshell, *Asian Tapas* is an invitation to explore the diverse cuisines covering the length and breadth of Asia. From Shanghai to Kyoto, and Mumbai to Singapore—these recipes take you on a remarkable journey through Asian food cultures that have already become such an integral part of our lives. There is plenty to spark the imagination here, and any cook with a wok hanging on the wall, a spice grinder on the shelf and a passion for fragrant herbs, aromatic spices and an abundance of fresh produce will find this a fascinating tour de force.

It doesn't matter whether you know your lemongrass from your galangal yet—if authors Christophe Megel, Anton Kilayko and the rest of the team at the Ritz-Carlton, Millennia Singapore have anything to do with it, you soon will. In *Asian Tapas*, they have taken up the challenge to develop an irresistible collection of new Asian recipes to fit our modern lifestyle. And how perfectly this book meets our needs! The very fact that the dishes are based on fresh seasonal ingredients—a characteristic of Asian cooking spawned from the necessity in earlier times to buy pro-

duce from the market daily—signals that this food is good for us. But the appeal is far greater than that. The recipes remind us that one of the main attractions of Asian cooking is the ability to assault each and every one of the senses simultaneously. Who does not enjoy hearing the sizzle of garlic in a hot pan or inhaling the heady fragrances of spices as they unfold? The combination of textures and colors and the exquisite range of tastes—by turns salty, sweet, sour or spicy—titillate our taste buds in unique ways. Within these pages you will find a skillfully concocted selection of recipes inspired by the traditional flavors of Thailand, Singapore, Vietnam, India, Japan and Bali, to name a few, but creatively updated for today's palates and cooking methods.

From the rustic Japanese *izakaya* pub tradition, Anton and Christophe have drawn small, delicate sushi and yakitori dishes, while from the elaborate *kaiseki* banquet tradition of Kyoto where tiny, exquisitely-presented dishes are slowly enjoyed with copious amount of sake (and this is also incidentally the home of the *bento* box)—they have been inspired to create refined beef and seafood delicacies to die for. The resulting recipes for Tataki Salmon Rolls topped with creamy cauliflower mousse and Japanese Beef Salad Rolls—simply constructed with tender strips of melt-in-the-mouth Kobe beef enclosing crisp, fresh vegetables—are delicious examples of the authors' innovative stance on traditional Asian ideas.

Insightful reference is given to Indian snacks traditions through dishes such as Fragrant

Khandvi Rolls made from quickly-prepared sheets of chickpea batter richly spiced and flavored with coconut and perfect served warm with drinks, and spicy Cheese Tikki Patties traditionally purchased from street vendors, made here with cream cheese and a touch of coriander.

From their local Singaporean haunts we find new twists on the honest fare found at hawker stalls. Think succulent beef or pork satays served with a spicy peanut sauce, Honey Glazed Chicken Wings packed with mushrooms and spices—and tasty Steamed Dim Sum Chicken Buns spiked with ginger and best served with tiny cups of piping-hot Chinese tea.

We travel to Vietnam, the original home of the delicate rice paper roll, and are presented with contemporary versions that have other flavors ingeniously woven into them. Rice Paper Sashimi Salad Rolls contain a lavish assortment of seafood served with an invigorating wasabi-based dip, while vegetarians will love a meatless version featuring sundried tomatoes and olives with tofu and shiitake mushrooms—both make perfect candidates to accompany pre-dinner cocktails.

From all these we learn how ageless Asian flavors and techniques can be transformed to fulfill our growing desire for food that is simple and easy to prepare yet still provides a jolt to the senses. Christophe Megel demonstrates innate talent as he serves up powerfully exciting new dishes for a variety of occasions. It is also to his great credit that he is bold enough to leap over culinary boundaries to borrow tastes from other corners of the globe while remaining true to the original

Asian flavors. His Salmon Avocado Sushi adds a hint of Mexican guacamole to a Japanese favorite and makes perfect sense while demonstrating his confidence and desire to have fun with food. The influences of France and Spain should come as no surprise in his Fougasse Bread with Thai Basil or his paella-inspired Saffron Sushi Rice Balls with fresh clams and chorizo sausage, but it is also plain to see that French-born Megel's time in Japan and Singapore has been well spent absorbing the cuisines on his doorstep. His signature pan-fried Crisp Asparagus Rolls in filo pastry with a sprinkling of parmesan cheese and tangy XO sauce inside—and his unforgettably delicious Bok Choy and Goat Cheese Barbajuans inspired by the Monegasque *barbajuans* served at Alain Ducasse's legendary Louis XV restaurant in Monte Carlo—have literally got his Ritz-Carlton patrons queuing up for more. His skills combined with those of Anton Kilayko—who I know from personal experience has exceptional knowledge of the local cuisines and an excellent grip on what appeals to today's palate—provide us with a truly unique collection of ideas.

What are Asian tapas? The word *tapas* (which means "lid") comes from the Spanish practice of covering drinks served in bars with a small saucer or a piece of bread to keep pesky flies at bay. The more enterprising establishments began to dress their "lids" with tasty morsels, and over time the idea developed into providing hungry patrons with a bountiful succession of bite-sized snacks to keep them seated and ordering more drinks. The word *tapas* seamlessly describes its

Asian snack and light meal counterparts and is a stroke of brilliance that has been used to succinctly express the modern style of Asian food found in this book.

Serving suggestions: The rule is—there is no set rule as to how and when, from sunrise to sunset, to serve any of the recipes in this book. In every manner and sense, these recipes are as versatile as they can be. Such treats as silky-textured Steamed Chicken Meatballs or Baked Kangkong Wonton Rolls can be as successfully served at a party or as a snack or a stylish appetizer. Mussels Steamed in Fragrant Coconut Cream redolent of curry, lemongrass and lime, or perhaps bold Balinese Beef Satays makes a good, quick al fresco lunch, but can also be served as supper for two. For formal dinners, consider dishes steeped in special flavors—like Steamed Fish with Sweet Mango and Herbs that features peppermint, coriander, basil and parsley or the Spicy Lamb Seekh Kebabs served on cinnamon sticks—while intriguing finger foods for parties or banquets can be created from recipes for Beef Yakitori with Eggplant, bite-sized portions of Asparagus Crab Salad with Ginger Cream or succulent Flaky Siew Mai Croissants. The manner in which you present your dishes is, again, entirely up to you. This food is so attractive and versatile, it can either be arranged in a simple, rustic bowl or a white platter or you can choose to take a more elegant and creative approach as shown in the stunning photographs that accompany these recipes.

rainbow quail eggs

Impressive to look at and extremely easy to put together, this recipe is great when you need cocktail canapés in a hurry. The salt-and-pepper flavors of the seaweed, *sancho* pepper and *nori* compliment the creamy eggs brilliantly and the various colors used are most striking.

6 cups (1$^1/_2$ liters) water
1 tablespoon salt
1 teaspoon white vinegar
24 quail eggs
1 tablespoon *nori* flakes (see note)
1 tablespoon *sancho* pepper (see note)
  or $^1/_2$ tablespoon paprika and $^1/_2$
  tablespoon ground red pepper
1 tablespoon purple seaweed

1 Bring the water, salt and vinegar to a boil in a saucepan over high heat. Add the eggs and boil for 3 minutes. Remove and plunge the eggs in cold water for several minutes to cool. Peel and set aside.
2 Cut a thin layer from the base of each egg to enable it to stand upright.
3 Coat 8 eggs with the *nori* flakes, 8 eggs with the *sancho* pepper and 8 eggs with the purple seaweed. Serve the quail eggs in a platter.

Note: *Nori* flakes and purple seaweed are different varieties of seaweeds seasoned with sweetened soy sauce. *Sancho* pepper is the peppery powder made from the ground leaves of the prickly ash plant (the taste is similar to Sichuan pepper, which may be used as a substitute). Often used for flavoring, these can be purchased in small bottles from Japanese supermarkets and Asian food stores.

Makes 24 eggs   Preparation time: 15 minutes   Cooking time: 15 minutes

chili and garlic herb marinated olives

A vibrant blend of rosemary, chili, citrus and garlic transforms a simple bowl of olives into a veritable fiesta. A perfect pre-dinner nibble, this takes no time at all to prepare.

2 cups (7 oz/200 g) black Kalamata olives
1$\frac{1}{2}$ cups (5 oz/150 g) green pitted olives (see note)
Rosemary leaves, to garnish
Coriander leaves (cilantro), to garnish

Spicy Dressing
1 tablespoon olive oil
2 tablespoons minced red chilies
5 cloves garlic, minced
3 tablespoons minced shallots
1 teaspoon rosemary leaves
2 tablespoons lime juice
2 tablespoons lemon juice
$\frac{1}{4}$ cup (60 ml) water
1 tablespoon rice wine or sake
1 to 2 teaspoons sugar
$\frac{1}{2}$ teaspoon fish sauce
1 teaspoon minced rosemary leaves

1 To make the Spicy Dressing, heat the olive oil in a skillet over medium heat and stir-fry the chilies, garlic and shallots until fragrant, about 1 minute. Add all the other ingredients and simmer for about 6 minutes, until the mixture has thickened and the sauce has reduced to $\frac{1}{4}$ the volume. Set aside.

2 Mix both types of olives in a salad bowl. Add the Spicy Dressing and toss to combine. Serve garnished with rosemary and coriander leaves.

Note: Fresh pitted olives, which are not so salty, are ideal for this dish. Alternatively, you may also use canned pitted olives and make the Spicy Dressing with double the amount of lemon juice, olive oil, sugar and fish sauce (other ingredients remain the same).

Makes 12 cocktail portions   Preparation time: 15 minutes
Cooking time: 7 minutes

pink martini

Ice cubes
1$\frac{1}{2}$ fl oz (45 ml) vodka
$\frac{1}{2}$ fl oz (15 ml) cherry brandy
$\frac{1}{3}$ fl oz (10 ml) crème de cacao white
Dash of grenadine syrup
Cherries, to garnish

Place ice cubes in a martini shaker. Add all the ingredients and shake vigorously, then strain into a martini glass and garnish with cherries on the rim.

Makes 1   Preparation time: 1 minute

scallop ceviche with xo sauce

Generally associated with Latin cuisine, a version of ceviche exists in the Spanish-influenced Philippines. Common to all ceviches is the technique of "cooking" raw seafood in acid citrus juices; here, Hong Kong's famous XO sauce (which includes dried scallops in its ingredients list) adds a truly modern Asian twist.

4 teaspoons lime juice
$1/2$ teaspoon Chicken Rice Chili Sauce
  (page 155)
$1/4$ teaspoon salt
$1/4$ teaspoon freshly ground black
  pepper
$1/4$ teaspoon sesame oil
$3/4$ in (2 cm) fresh young ginger root,
  sliced into thin shreds
4 large fresh scallops
3 teaspoons XO sauce

1 Combine the lime juice with the Chicken Rice Chili Sauce, salt, pepper, sesame oil and ginger in a bowl, and mix well.
2 Cut each scallop horizontally into 3 thin disks. Marinate the disks in the lime juice and chili mixture for about 15 minutes.
3 Serve the scallop disks on individual spoons, topped with $1/4$ teaspoon of the XO sauce and a few strands of shredded ginger from the marinade. Serve cold.

Makes 12 cocktail portions   Preparation time: 15 minutes

spicy lamb seekh kebabs

The heady scent of dried spice pervades this quickly-prepared lamb dish. Forming the mixture around cinnamon sticks and then baking adds another jolt of flavor—for a more exotic presentation though, trying using the kiwi fruit vine instead (as shown in photo).

10 oz (300 g) ground lamb
$^1/_2$ teaspoon ground cumin
$^1/_2$ teaspoon ground coriander
1 teaspoon ground red pepper
1 teaspoon salt
1 teaspoon grated fresh ginger
1 small green chili, minced
4 cloves garlic, minced
16 long cinnamon sticks (3 in/8 cm each) or kiwi fruit vine, to use as skewers

Spice Powder
2 star anise
2 black cardamom pods
4 green cardamom pods
1 blade mace
6 cloves

1 Preheat the oven to 400°F (200°C).
2 Make the Spice Powder first by dry-roasting the ingredients in a non-stick skillet for about 1 minute, stirring constantly until fragrant. Grind the ingredients in a spice grinder to get 3 teaspoons of Spice Powder. Sift out the large pieces to yield 2 teaspoons of fine Spice Powder.
3 Combine the ground lamb with the sifted Spice Powder, cumin, coriander, red pepper, salt, ginger, chili and garlic in a large bowl and mix well. Divide the lamb mixture into 16 equal portions. Wrap each portion around a cinnamon stick. Repeat the process until the lamb mixture is used up.
4 Place the lamb kebabs on a baking tray and bake for 8 minutes. Alternatively, you may form little sausage rolls with the lamb mixture and pan-fry them in a skillet with 1 tablespoon of olive oil over medium-high heat for 5 minutes or until cooked. Serve hot.

Makes 16 kebabs   Preparation time: 20 minutes   Cooking time: 10 minutes

salmon avocado sushi

Avocado and salmon make a heavenly match, their lush textures and delicate flavors melting together, with pastel-colored results. Here they combine in a novel interpretation of sushi which, while looking every bit as spectacular as traditional versions, is much easier to prepare and construct.

3 oz (100 g) salmon fillets
Wakame seaweed or salad greens to
    garnish (optional)

Avocado Filling
1 large ripe avocado, peeled, pit
    removed, flesh diced (see note)
1 small white onion, diced
1 small tomato, blanched, peeled and
    deseeded, flesh diced
1 lemon, halved
2 to 3 teaspoons wasabi paste or hot
    Chinese mustard
$1/_4$ teaspoon salt

1 To make the Avocado Filling, squeeze the juice from $1/_2$ of the lemon over the avocado cubes in a bowl and toss lightly to mix, then add the onion and tomato. Add the wasabi or mustard and salt, squeeze the other $1/_2$ of the lemon over it and toss until well combined. Set aside.
2 Slice the salmon fillets into 12 thin strips, each measuring 1 x 5 in (3 x 12 cm). Spoon 1 teaspoon of the Avocado Filling onto each salmon strip and roll one end up tightly until both ends meet.
3 To serve, lay a small bed of the wakame seaweed or salad greens (if using) on a serving dish and top with a salmon roll.

Note: To prepare an avocado, slice the avocado lengthwise around the pit, then gently rotate to separate. Carefully strike the pit with a sharp knife, turn the knife clockwise and anticlockwise to remove the pit. Scoop the flesh out whole or in parts using a spoon. If not using immediately, squeeze some lemon or lime juice over the flesh to prevent discoloration.

Makes 12 portions   Preparation time: 30 minutes

fresh oysters with ginger and lemongrass ponzu

Spanking-fresh oysters really are at their absolute best if you take the trouble to shuck them yourself. That process is critical to this recipe in order to collect the precious juices—which form the basis of a shimmering jelly that tops each luscious oyster.

18 fresh unshucked oysters
1/3 cup (125 g) thinly sliced fresh young ginger root
3 stalks lemongrass, thick bottom third only, outer layers discarded, inner part bruised
1 tablespoon Japanese soy sauce
6 tablespoons *ponzu* sauce
1/4 teaspoon ground white pepper
1 cup (250 ml) water
2 gelatin leaves or 1/2 tablespoon gelatin powder
Large bowl of ice cubes
Tobiko roe or salmon roe, to garnish
Finely grated lime zest, to garnish

1 Brush the oysters vigorously under running water to remove sand and dirt. Shuck each oyster by holding it firmly in one hand with the deeper half of the shell underneath. Insert the blade of an oyster knife into the hinged side of the shells and gently turn the knife to pry open the shells enough to sever the hinge muscle. Once the muscle is cut, slide the knife between the shells to open, catching the oyster juice in a bowl or pan. The flesh should still be attached to the deeper shell. Discard the shallow top shell. Shuck all the oysters in this manner. Strain the juice into a small saucepan. Keep the oysters in their shells in the refrigerator.
2 Add the ginger, lemongrass, soy sauce, *ponzu*, pepper and water to the reserved oyster juice and bring the mixture to a boil over medium heat. Reduce heat to low and simmer until the mixture has reduced to half, about 10 minutes. Remove and discard the ginger and lemongrass. Transfer the mixture to a small bowl.
3 If using gelatin leaves, briefly soak them in water to soften, then remove. Add the softened gelatin leaves (or gelatin powder) to the oyster juice mixture, stir well and place the bowl on top of a large bowl of ice cubes to cool for about 3 minutes, stirring constantly, until it thickens to a loose jelly.
4 Remove the oysters from the refrigerator, spoon 1 tablespoon of the jelly over each one and garnish with a dollop of tobiko roe or salmon roe and a sprinkling of grated lime zest.

Makes 18 oysters   Preparation time: 20 minutes   Cooking time: 15 minutes

steamed fish with sweet mango and herbs

The succulence of ripe mango, the aromas of peppermint, coriander and parsley and the unmistakable presence of chili, sweet soy and vinegar, elevate the humble steamed fish to the status of a memorable and heavenly dish.

1 ripe mango (about 5 oz/150 g), peeled and pitted, flesh diced
6 shallots, minced
$^1/_4$ teaspoon chili oil
1 red chili, deseeded and very thinly sliced
2 tablespoons minced spring onions
3 tablespoons minced coriander leaves (cilantro)
3 tablespoons minced parsley leaves
$^1/_2$ teaspoon minced peppermint
10 oz (300 g) cod fish, seabass or sole fillets
$^1/_4$ teaspoon salt
$^1/_4$ teaspoon ground white pepper
2 Chinese cabbage leaves or any other large green vegetable leaves, for steaming

Dipping Sauce
1 tablespoon sweet black soy sauce
1 tablespoon rice vinegar
1 tablespoon *yuzu* or mixture of mandarin orange and lime juice

1 To make the Dipping Sauce, combine all the ingredients in a bowl, mix well and set aside.

2 Place the diced mango, shallots, chili oil, chili, spring onions, coriander leaves, parsley and peppermint in a large bowl and mix until well combined. Set aside.

3 Carefully slice the fish fillets horizontally with a very sharp knife into thin sheets about $^1/_8$ in (3 mm) thick. Spoon some of the mango mixture on top of each slice and roll it up into a small log. Repeat until all the slices are used up and top each roll with a sprinkling of salt and pepper.

4 Line a steamer with the cabbage leaves or other green leaves, then place the fish rolls on top and steam over high heat for about 3 minutes. Serve hot with the Dipping Sauce.

Makes 8 rolls   Preparation time: 15 minutes   Cooking time: 3 minutes

tataki salmon rolls with cauliflower mousse

Tataki is a dish of Japanese origin, usually involving prime beef, very quickly seared on the outside and left meltingly "blue" on the inside. Fresh salmon is another prime candidate for this treatment; here, it is formed into neat cylinders and topped with a lush, creamy cauliflower purée.

1 lb (500 g) fresh salmon fillets
1 teaspoon salt
1 teaspoon ground white pepper
4 tablespoons olive oil
1 large head of cauliflower (1 lb/500 g), stems discarded and florets trimmed to yield 9 cups ($2^1/_4$ liters) of tender cauliflower florets
4 tablespoons (80 g) unsalted butter
3 tablespoons fresh cream
1 teaspoon black sesame seeds
1 daikon (about 1 lb/500 g)
2 oz (60 g) caviar
Garlic chives and sliced chili, to garnish

Step-by-step photos and instructions for this recipe are provided on the opposite page.

1 Slice the salmon fillets lengthwise into 3 long, narrow pieces and season with $^1/_2$ of the salt and pepper. Place the skillet over high heat and add the olive oil. When the oil is smoking hot, sear the salmon fillets for 3 seconds on each side. Remove the salmon from the pan and pat with paper towels to remove excess oil. Roll each piece up tightly with 3 layers of plastic wrap. While holding the ends of the plastic wrap, roll the salmon on top of a cutting board to form a cylinder. Twist the ends of the plastic wrap tightly to fasten. Repeat with the other two pieces of salmon fillets. Chill in the ice water for 5 minutes or refrigerator for $^1/_2$ an hour.
2 Blanch the cauliflower florets for 3 to 5 minutes until soft. Remove and drain in a colander. Purée the cooked cauliflower in a blender with the butter, cream, sesame seeds, remaining salt and pepper until smooth. Set aside.
3 Peel the daikon and trim the ends away. Trim off the sides and shave 18 very thin daikon sheets using a vegetable shaver. Each sheet should measure about 3 x 6 in (8 x 15 cm). Set aside.
4 Remove the plastic wrap from the salmon rolls and slice them into pieces. Each piece should measure $^1/_2$ the width of the daikon sheets (about $1^1/_2$ in/4 cm). To assemble, stand each piece of the salmon upright and wrap a daikon sheet tightly around it like a belt. Top the empty half with some cauliflower mousse using a piping bag or tiny spoon, then garnish with a dollop of caviar and chives spear as shown. Serve cold on a platter.

Note: The daikon sheets should stick when rolled around the salmon pieces. If they don't, the problem is usually that they are too thick and stiff. Try cutting thinner ones, or dab a tiny bit of constarch paste under the end to glue it down.

Makes 18 pieces   Preparation time: 1 hour   Cooking time: 5 minutes

1. Slice the salmon fillets into 3 long, narrow pieces, then season with the salt and pepper.

2. Sear the salmon pieces for 3 seconds on each side.

3. Roll each piece of the salmon tightly with 3 layers of plastic wrap to form a cylinder and twist the ends of the plastic wrap tightly to fasten.

4. Chill the wrapped salmon in a bowl of ice water or refrigerator.

5. Peel and trim the ends of the daikon and shave into thin sheets with a vegetable shaver.

6. Trim each sheet of daikon to a 3 x 6-in (8 x 15-cm) rectangle.

7. Remove the plastic wrap and slice the salmon rolls into pieces. Each piece should measure $1/2$ the width of the daikon sheets.

8. Stand each salmon piece upright and wrap a daikon sheet tightly around it like a belt.

9. Fold a piece of baking paper into a cone to make a piping bag and fill it with the cauliflower mousse.

10. Fill the top half with cauliflower mousse, pushing downward gently.

grilled chicken and fish tandoori strips

Gently spiced tandoori-grilled meats and fish are universally popular. This versatile recipe, which works equally well with chicken or fish, owes its depth of flavor and tender results to overnight marination in an aromatic mixture of spices, coconut cream and lime juice, followed by quick grilling.

10 oz (300 g) boneless and skinless chicken breasts
5 oz (150 g) white fish fillets (like snapper or cod)
Lime wedges, to serve

Marinade
3 teaspoons tandoori spice powder (see note) or 1 teaspoon *garam masala*
1 tablespoon fish sauce
1 tablespoon rice vinegar or white vinegar
4 tablespoons coconut cream
4 cloves garlic, crushed
3 tablespoons minced coriander leaves (cilantro)
1 tablespoon freshly minced red chili or 2 teaspoons ground red pepper
2 teaspoons lime juice
1 teaspoon salt
1 teaspoon freshly ground black pepper
1 teaspoon sugar
1 teaspoon ground coriander

1 Make the Marinade by combining all the ingredients in a bowl. Divide the Marinade into 2 bowls, place the chicken in one and the fish in the other. Cover and marinate overnight in the refrigerator.
2 Grill the chicken for 4 minutes on each side, and the fish for 2 minutes on each side, or until done.
3 Cut the chicken and fish into bite-sized pieces and serve immediately with lime wedges.

Note: Tandoori spice powder is a hot blend of spices used in Indian cuisine, which usually includes ground chilies, *garam masala*, turmeric, saffron and red food coloring. It can be purchased ready-made from Asian grocery stores and good supermarkets or you can make your own at home if preferred.

Makes 24 fish pieces and 18 chicken pieces   Preparation time: 20 minutes + marination time   Cooking time: 45 minutes

coriander ginger shrimp with sweet thai chili sauce

Minced fresh coriander leaves (cilantro) and piquant ginger lend their perfume to a crunchy coating for tender seafood; a splash of sweet Thai chili sauce is the perfect embellishment. The presentation of this dish, designed for passing around at a drinks party, is as beautiful as it is practical.

1 tablespoon lemon or lime juice
24 fresh jumbo shrimp, tiger prawns or crayfish (about 1 lb/500 g), peeled and deveined
2 cups (80 g) breadcrumbs
$1/2$ teaspoon salt
$1/2$ teaspoon ground white pepper
4 tablespoons minced coriander leaves (cilantro)
1 teaspoon minced fresh ginger root
2 egg yolks, beaten
4 teaspoons olive oil
12 bamboo skewers (optional)
$1/3$ cup sweet Thai chili sauce, for dipping (see note)

Sweet Thai Chili Sauce
$1/2$ cup white vinegar
$1/2$ cup (100 g) sugar
5 cloves garlic, minced
3 to 5 red chilies, deseeded and minced
$1/2$ teaspoon salt

1 To make the Sweet Thai Chili Sauce, mix all the ingredients in a saucepan and bring to a boil over high heat. Reduce heat to low and simmer until the sauce thickens slightly, about 15 to 20 minutes. Set aside.
2 Rub the lemon or lime juice onto the shrimp or prawns. Set aside.
3 Combine the breadcrumbs, salt, pepper, coriander leaves and ginger in a bowl and mix well.
4 Dip each shrimp or prawn in the egg yolks, then roll it in the breadcrumbs mixture to coat. Coat all the shrimp or prawns in this manner.
5 Heat the olive oil in a skillet over medium heat and pan-fry the coated shrimp or prawns, a few at a time, for about 2 minutes on each side. Remove and drain on paper towels. Skewer the shrimp on bamboo skewers if desired and serve hot with dipping bowls of sweet Thai chilli sauce.

Note: Sweet Thai chili sauce (*nahm jim*) is sold bottled in Asian food stores, but it is very easy to make fresh using this recipe.

Makes 12 sticks or serves 4   Preparation time: 30 minutes
Cooking time: 10 minutes

flaky siew mai croissants

Siew Mai pork and shrimp dumplings have long been a favorite *dim sum* offering. Here, in an inspired departure from tradition, crisp, flaky croissant dough stands in for the usual steamed wonton wrappers and the results are positively addictive.

Flour, for dusting
4 sheets frozen puff pastry (11 x 24 in/27 x 60 cm) or croissant dough, defrosted for 2 to 3 hours before using
1 egg white
Black sesame seeds, to garnish

Siew Mai Filling
5 oz (150 g) ground pork
4 oz (125 g) ground chicken
4 fresh shiitake mushrooms, stems removed and discarded, caps diced
5 oz (150 g) fresh shrimp or prawns, peeled, deveined and ground to a paste in a food processor
$1/2$ teaspoon salt
$1/2$ teaspoon sugar
$1/2$ teaspoon ground white pepper
$1/2$ teaspoon chicken stock powder (bouillon powder)
$1/2$ teaspoon flour
1 egg
1 egg yolk

1 Preheat the oven to 400°F (200°C).
2 To make the Siew Mai Filling, combine all the ingredients in a bowl and mix until well blended and smooth. Set aside.
3 Unroll each puff pastry or croissant dough on a lightly floured surface and roll it into an 11 x 24-in (27 x 60-cm) rectangle, $1/8$ in (3 mm) thick if necessary. Cut out approximately 7 equilateral triangles, each with a base measuring 4 in (10 cm), marking the base of the triangles along the length of the pastry sheet. Cut out a total of 25 triangles from all the pastry sheets.
4 Place 1 tablespoon of the Siew Mai Filling on the base of each triangle and roll the base over the Siew Mai Filling, then roll up tightly into a cylinder, brushing the tip of the triangle with a bit of the egg white to seal. Repeat with the remaining pastry and Filling.
5 Brush the top of each croissant with egg white and sprinkle with sesame seeds. Bake in the oven at 400°F (200°C) for 20 minutes. Arrange on a platter and serve hot.

Note: If the puff pastry is not available in this size, just roll it out to a $1/8$ in (3 mm) thick rectangle and cut out as many 4-in (10-cm) base equilateral triangles with a height measuring 11 in (27 cm).

Makes 25 croissants   Preparation time: 1 hour   Cooking time: 20 minutes

baby vegetable crudités with spicy yuzu dressing

Creamy, home-made mayonnaise served as a dressing for crisp, baby vegetables (*crudités*) is a French idea but the punchy flavors used here—chili, coriander and *yuzu*—are pure Asia. Simple to prepare, this light and sophisticated dish makes perfect summertime fare.

3 fennel roots, cut into quarters lengthwise
5 baby carrots, halved lengthwise
1 bell pepper, deseeded and cut into quarters lengthwise
2 heads Belgian endive, cut into quarters lengthwise
3 baby cucumbers, cut into sticks
6 to 8 baby asparagus spears, bottom ends trimmed and discarded

Spicy Yuzu Dressing
1 bird's-eye chili, minced
2 cloves garlic, minced
1 tablespoon *yuzu* juice (see note)
2 teaspoons minced coriander leaves (cilantro)
2 teaspoons minced spring onion
$^1/_4$ cup (60 ml) olive oil
1 teaspoon dijon mustard
1 egg yolk
$^1/_2$ teaspoon salt

1 To make the Spicy Yuzu Dressing, combine the chili, garlic, *yuzu*, coriander leaves, spring onion and $^1/_4$ teaspoon of the olive oil in a mortar or blender and grind to form a smooth paste. Combine with the mustard and egg yolk in a medium-sized bowl. Stir the mixture in one direction with a whisk, adding the remaining olive oil, a teaspoon at a time, until the oil emulsifies with the mixture. Season with the salt.
2 Serve the vegetable sticks in a salad bowl with a dipping bowl of the Spicy Yuzu Dressing on the side.

Note: *Yuzu* is a mild Japanese citrus with a delicate fragrance, similar to a tart mandarin orange or quince. If not available, use a mixture of mandarin orange and lemon juice in equal portions instead. Lemon juice sweetened with a sprinkling of sugar is also a good substitute.

Serves 8   Preparation time: 20 minutes

bok choy and goat cheese barbajuans

Delectable crunchy and light puffs, their filling a bold combination of goat cheese, mushrooms, ginger, coriander and bok choy, are a true East-meets-West creation. This seemingly unlikely mix—which is based on the MONEGASQUE *barbajuans* works brilliantly, resulting in intense, lingering flavors.

4 cups (600 g) flour
$^1/_2$ teaspoon salt
$^1/_2$ cup (125 ml) olive oil
$^1/_2$ cup (125 ml) water
1 egg, beaten
Oil for deep-frying

Filling
1 tablespoon olive oil
2 cloves garlic, minced
$1^1/_2$ cups (80 g) chopped baby bok choy
1 teaspoon salt
1 teaspoon ground white pepper
8 fresh shiitake mushrooms, stems removed and discarded, caps diced
$^1/_2$ cup (200 g) cooked rice
2 tablespoons goat cheese
1 tablespoon grated parmesan cheese
$^1/_2$ teaspoon grated fresh ginger
2 tablespoons minced coriander leaves (cilantro)
1 egg, beaten

Step-by-step photos and instructions for this recipe are provided on page 42.

1 Sift $2^1/_2$ cups (400 g) of the flour with the salt into a mixing bowl and make a well in the center. Pour in $^1/_2$ of the olive oil and knead well with the hands, adding the water gradually, until the dough is smooth and elastic. Sprinkle a clean flat surface with the flour and continue to knead the dough for 2 minutes. Shape the dough into a ball, wrap with plastic wrap and refrigerate for 3 hours.

2 To make the Filling, heat $^1/_2$ of the olive oil in a skillet over medium heat and stir-fry the garlic and bok choy with $^1/_2$ of the salt and the pepper for 1 minute. Transfer the bok choy to a bowl and set aside. Heat the remaining olive oil in the skillet and stir-fry the shiitake mushrooms with the remaining salt and pepper for 1 minute. Remove from heat and transfer to a bowl. Add the bok choy, rice, goat cheese, parmesan cheese, ginger, coriander leaves and egg, tossing gently to combine.

3 Once the dough is well chilled, divide it into 2 portions. On a lightly floured surface, roll out 1 portion of the chilled dough to $^1/_8$-in (3-mm) thickness and trim to obtain a long, narrow rectangular sheet measuring 15 x 5 in (37 x 12 cm). Spoon 1 tablespoon of the Filling at equal intervals along the length of the dough, placing them slightly closer to one end as shown in the photos on page 42. Brush the dough all around each mound of Filling with the beaten egg. Cut the dough vertically into 2 sections for easy folding.

4 To enclose the Filling for each section, lift the length of the dough sheet gently over the mounds of Filling and press the 2 ends together, then press the dough gently all around each individual mound to seal. Cut to separate each mound and trim with a pastry cutter to obtain square puffs. Dust away excess flour before frying.

5 Deep-fry the puffs in very hot oil for 3 minutes each until golden brown. Serve warm.

Makes 10 puffs   Preparation time: 45 minutes + 3 hours chilling
Cooking time: 6 minutes

bok choy and goat cheese barbajuans

1. Knead the dough into a ball, wrap with plastic wrap and refrigerate for 3 hours.

2. On a floured surface, divide the dough into 2 portions. Roll out each portion to $^1/_8$ in (3 mm) thick and trim to obtain 15 x 5-in (37 x 12-cm) rectangles.

3. Spoon 1 tablespoon of the Filling at equal intervals along the length of the dough slightly closer to one end.

4. Brush the dough all round each mound with the beaten egg.

6. Fold the dough sheet over the Filling and press gently all around each mound to seal.

7-8. Trim with a pastry cutter to obtain square puffs and remove excess flour before frying.

5. Cut the dough vertically into 2 sections for easy folding.

flaky cashew nut puff pastry squares

1. Make the Oil Dough by beating the butter and flour until smooth, then chill for 2 hours.

2. Make the Base Dough by combining all the ingredients in a bowl. Knead for 5 minutes until smooth. Chill for 1 hour.

3. Roll out the Base Dough to a 1/8 in (3 mm) thick rectangle. Roll out the Oil Dough to half the size.

4. Place the Oil Dough on one side of the Base Dough and fold to form a "sandwich".

5. Press the dough "sandwich" lightly, then flatten by beating it with a rolling pin.

6. Fold one third of the flattened dough "sandwich" to the middle, then fold the other end over it.

7. Roll the dough out in one direction to form a rectangle 1/2 in (1 cm) thick. Repeat step 6 and 7 three more times.

8. Fold both sides of the dough sheet from either end to meet at the middle, then fold it in half to form a thick stack.

9. Cut the stack of dough into 2, flatten each half by beating it with a rolling pin. Roll to form a rectangle 1/4 in (5 mm) thick and chill for 1 hour in the freezer.

10. Heat the oven and prepare the icing. Spread a thin layer of the icing on top of each dough sheet.

11. Using a pastry knife, cut the dough into 1 x 2 1/2-in (2 1/2 x 6-cm) rectangles.

12. Top each rectangle with cashew nut halves and bake in the oven at 300°F (150°C).

flaky cashew nut puff pastry squares

This dough is prepared in much the same way as puff pastry; the butter produces many delicate layers that give the puffs their characteristic "lift" and flaky lightness. Whipped icing, a drizzle of raspberry purée and some cashew nuts are the only adornments necessary for this spectacular dessert.

1 egg white
2 cups icing sugar
$1/4$ cup (60 g) dry-roasted unsalted
    cashew nuts, halved
Raspberry purée, as topping (optional)

Oil Dough
6 tablespoons (125 g) butter
1 cup (150 g) flour

Base Dough
$1^1/4$ cups (175 g) flour
3 tablespoons (60 g) shortening
1 cup (250 ml) water

Step-by-step photos and instructions for this recipe are provided on page 43.

1 To make the Oil Dough, beat the butter and flour until smooth with a mixer at slow speed for 2 minutes. Transfer to a tray or bowl, cover with a cloth or plastic wrap and chill in the refrigerator for 2 hours.

2 To make the Dough, combine all the ingredients in a bowl and mix together, then transfer to a floured surface and knead for about 5 minutes until smooth. Place the dough in a bowl, cover with a damp cloth or plastic wrap and chill in the refrigerator for 1 hour.

3 Once the Base Dough is well chilled, roll it on a floured surface into a rectangle $1/8$ in (3 mm) thick and set aside. Roll the Oil Dough to a similar shape that is approximately half the size of the Base Dough. Place the Oil Dough sheet on top of one half of the Base Dough sheet and fold the other half of the Base Dough sheet over it. Press the combined dough "sandwich" lightly to seal and flatten by beating it with a rolling pin until it is about $1/2$ in (1 cm) thick.

4 Fold one third of the flattened dough "sandwich" to the middle, then fold the other end over it. Roll it out in one direction to form a rectangle $1/2$ in (1 cm) thick. Repeat this folding and rolling process 3 more times, flouring the dough or surface as necessary.

5 Fold both sides of the rectangular dough sheet from either end to meet at the middle, then fold it in half to form a thick stack. Cut the stack of dough into 2, then flatten each half by beating it with a rolling pin. Roll out to form a rectangle $1/4$ in (5 mm) thick. Chill the dough for 1 hour in the freezer.

6 Preheat the oven to 300°F (150°C).

7 Beat the egg white and icing sugar with a mixer until stiff. When the dough is well chilled and firm, spread a thin layer of the icing on top with a spatula. Cut the dough into 1 x $2^1/2$ in ($2^1/2$ x 6 cm) rectangles and top each one with 3 cashew nut halves. Bake in the oven at 300°F (150°C) for 30 minutes. Serve, topped with raspberry purée (if using).

Makes 80 pieces   Preparation time: 45 minutes + 3 hours chilling
Cooking time: 30 minutes

fresh lobster mango skewers with sweet vanilla chili dressing

Fresh lobster and juicy sweet mango make a heavenly combination and the perfect dish for a celebration or party. In this stunning recipe, the pairing is made even more luxurious by the addition of vanilla bean seeds to the simple dressing.

8 cups (2 liters) water
1 teaspoon salt
1 teaspoon sugar
5 star anise
1 fresh lobster (about 1$3/_4$ lbs/850 g)
Ice water
1 large ripe mango (about 9 oz/250 g), peeled and cut into bite-sized chunks
10 small bamboo or stainless steel skewers
Daikon or mixed sprouts, to garnish
Coriander leaves (cilantro), to garnish
10 lemon wedges

Sweet Vanilla Chili Dressing
1 tablespoon bottled sweet chili sauce (see note)
1 tablespoon tomato ketchup
1 teaspoon olive oil
$1/_2$ teaspoon sesame oil
1 tablespoon sugar
1 tablespoon water
1 tablespoon lime juice
1 teaspoon minced coriander leaves (cilantro)
1 pod vanilla or 2 drops vanilla essence

1 To make the Sweet Vanilla Chili Dressing, combine the chili sauce, tomato ketchup, olive oil, sesame oil, sugar, water, lime juice and minced coriander leaves in a bowl. Slice open the vanilla pod and scrape out the seeds with a spoon. Add the seeds (or vanilla essence) to the mixture and stir to mix well. Set aside.

2 Bring the water to a boil in a pot over high heat and add the salt, sugar and star anise. Detach the claws from the lobster and boil the lobster and claws for 10 minutes, uncovered.

3 Drain the lobster and claws and plunge into ice water to cool. Remove and discard the head of the lobster and cut the body into two. Remove the flesh from the body and claws carefully. Do not break the flesh.

4 Slice the lobster meat into bite-sized chunks to obtain about 14 chunks from the body and 3 chunks from each claw. Thread 2 chunks of lobster and 2 chunks of mango onto each skewer.

5 Serve chilled in individual serving plates or bowls and spoon $1/_2$ teaspoon of Sweet Vanilla Chili Dressing over each skewer. Garnish each skewer with daikon or mixed sprouts, coriander leaves and a lemon wedge.

Note: The bottled sweet chili sauce called for in this recipe usually contains chili, vinegar, sugar, salt, ginger and garlic. It's easy to make up a little of your own sauce if you cannot find it or don't want to buy a whole bottle.

Makes 10 skewers   Preparation time: 30 minutes   Cooking time: 10 minutes

stuffed zucchini blossoms

Zucchini blossoms have a fragile beauty and are a real treat when in season. They are often served stuffed and the filling devised for this dish shows true innovation, with its arresting combination of goat cheese, Thai curry paste and ginger.

4 fresh zucchini blossoms or tiny bell
  peppers
4 tablespoons chicken stock or $1/4$ teaspoon chicken stock powder dissolved
  in 4 tablespoons hot water
1 tablespoon butter

Filling
2 teaspoons olive oil
1 tablespoon minced fresh ginger root
$1^1/_2$ cups (7 oz/200 g) diced bok choy
$1/_2$ cup (45 g) diced Chinese cabbage
$1/_2$ teaspoon salt
$1/_2$ teaspoon ground white pepper
2 fresh shiitake mushrooms, stems
  removed and discarded, caps sliced
4 oz (120 g) ground chicken, mixed with
  $1/_2$ teaspoon chicken stock powder
  (bouillon powder)
2 tablespoons goat cheese or ricotta
  cheese
1 teaspoon Thai green curry paste
1 egg yolk

1 To make the Filling, heat 1 teaspoon olive oil in a skillet over medium heat and stir-fry $1/_2$ of the ginger with the bok choy and Chinese cabbage for about 1 minute until barely cooked and then season with $1/_2$ of the salt and pepper. Remove and set aside. In the same manner, stir-fry the remaining ginger with the mushrooms and then season with the remaining salt and pepper. Chop the vegetables and mushrooms into small pieces and combine with the ground chicken in a bowl. Add the goat cheese or ricotta, green curry paste and egg yolk, and mix until well blended. Set aside.

2 Preheat the oven to 400°F (200°C).

3 Carefully reach inside the zucchini blossoms to snap off the stamens, taking care not to tear the petals apart. Stuff the zucchini blossoms with the Filling, pinching the tips of the flower petals together and lightly twist to keep the Filling within the flower petals. Cut long slits into the stems starting about 1 in ($2^1/_2$ cm) from the base of the petals, to ensure even cooking. If using bell peppers, cut into half and remove the seeds and white pith, and stuff with the Filling.

4 Place the stuffed zucchini blossoms or bell peppers, chicken stock and butter in a shallow casserole dish and bake in the oven at 400°F (200°C) for 10 to 15 minutes, basting the stuffed blossoms or peppers with the chicken stock occasionally. Serve warm.

Makes 4 portions   Preparation time: 30 minutes   Cooking time: 20 minutes

crisp cheese tikki patties

The essence of this dish lies in the use of mild Northern Indian spices and paneer, the fresh, creamy cheese so common in that region. With their crisp coating and soft, comforting fillings, tikkis make a superb casual appetizer or an inspired addition to an Indian-style buffet.

1 cup (250 ml) plain yoghurt, drained (see note)
1 cup (250 g) cream cheese or paneer
$1/2$ large red onion, diced
4 tablespoons minced green chilies
2 to 3 tablespoons minced fresh ginger root
2 teaspoons minced coriander leaves (cilantro)
$1/2$ to 1 teaspoon salt
$3/4$ cup chickpea flour (150 g) or bread-crumbs (45 g)
Oil for deep-frying

1 Combine the yoghurt and cream cheese or paneer in a bowl and mix well with the onion, chilies, ginger, coriander leaves and salt. Chill in the refigerator for 10 minutes to harden slightly.

2 Pour the chickpea flour or breadcrumbs into a medium bowl. Flour your hands, scoop 1 tablespoon of the cheese mixture and form it into a small patty. Coat the patty on all sides with the chickpea flour or breadcrumbs. Repeat until the cheese mixture is used up.

3 Deep-fry the patties in a wok or saucepan over high heat, turning constantly, for 1 minute or until golden brown. Drain on paper towels and serve hot.

Note: It is important to drain the yoghurt by pouring off the whey or liquid. You can do this by hanging the yoghurt for $1/2$ an hour in a piece of cloth or placing it in a paper filter and allowing the liquid to drain out. The patties can be prepared the day before and refrigerated before deep-frying.

Makes 24 pieces   Preparation time: 20 minutes   Cooking time: 5 minutes

japanese beef salad rolls

The best quality *kobe* or *wagyu* beef, lightly marbled with fat, is highly prized by the Japanese for its melt-in-the-mouth tenderness. A little goes a long way in this dish, where the meat's inherent richness contrasts nicely with the crispness of vegetables and the zen-like purity of a soy-based sauce.

4 oz (120 g) thinly sliced *wagyu* beef or
 sukiyaki beef (see note)
1 cup (250 ml) beef or veal stock or $^{1}/_{2}$
 beef stock cube dissolved in 1 cup
 (250 ml) hot water
$^{1}/_{2}$ carrot, cut into thin strips
$^{1}/_{2}$ zucchini, cut into thin strips
$^{1}/_{2}$ cup (20 g) alfalfa sprouts
$^{1}/_{2}$ cup (20 g) daikon sprouts

Sesame Dressing
2 tablespoons soy sauce
$^{1}/_{4}$ cup minced white onion
2 tablespoons beef or veal stock
2 tablespoons sake
$^{1}/_{2}$ tablespoon sesame paste

1 To make the Sesame Dressing, purée all the ingredients to a smooth paste using a hand blender or mortar. Set aside.
2 Briefly blanch the beef strips in the beef stock, about 10 seconds each.
3 Place 4 to 5 strips of carrot and zucchini with some daikon and alfalfa sprouts on a strip of beef and roll it up. Repeat the process until all the ingredients are used up. Serve the beef rolls individually with the Sesame Dressing.

Note: Sukiyaki beef works fine in this recipe if *wagyu* beef is not available. Sukiyaki beef is sold in Japanese supermarkets overseas—it is very high-quality beef that has been shaved into ultra-thin strips. If you cannot find it, buy a thick, well marbled steak and put it in the freezer wrapped in plastic wrap for about 1 hour until half frozen. Unwrap the steak and, using a very sharp knife, shave the steak lengthwise to obtain long, narrow strips about 6 x 1$^{1}/_{2}$ in (15 x 4 cm) and $^{1}/_{8}$ in (3 mm) thick.

Makes 10 rolls   Preparation time: 20 minutes   Cooking time: 1 minute

tangy pot stickers with ginger and garlic chives

Pot stickers derive their evocative name from the way they brown—they stick to their cooking pot as steaming liquid evaporates around them. You can purchase the wrappers required to make these; however making your own is easy and far more satisfying.

Water

3 tablespoons Black Chinese vinegar
2 in (5 cm) fresh ginger root, cut into tiny shreds, to garnish
1 spring onion, minced, to garnish

Dough

1 cup (150 g) flour, sifted
$1/2$ teaspoon salt
1 tablespoon lard or vegetable shortening
$1/4$ cup (60 ml) boiling water

Filling

2 teaspoons freshly grated horseradish
1 clove garlic, minced
$1/2$ tablespoon minced fresh ginger root
1 tablespoon minced lemongrass, taken from the inner part of the thick end of the stalk
2 slices pickled Japanese ginger
1 tablespoon black soy sauce
$1/2$ teaspoon dried shrimp paste
1 teaspoon salt
10 oz (300 g) ground pork
3 teaspoons minced garlic chives or Chinese chives

1 To make the Dough, combine the flour, salt and lard or shortening in a bowl. Gradually pour in the boiling water and mix to form a firm dough. Flour your hands and knead the dough until smooth and soft on a floured surface, then cover with a damp cloth and refrigerate for 1 hour.
2 To make the Filling, grind all the ingredients except the pork and chives to a smooth paste in a blender or food processor, then mix well with the ground pork and chives. Set aside.
3 Using a rolling pin, roll out the Dough on a floured surface until it is $1/8$ in (3 mm) thick and trim the edges to form a rectangle. Using a round cookie cutter, cut out $3^1/2$-in (9-cm) circles.
4 Spoon $3/4$ tablespoon of the Filling and roll it into a ball. Place the Filling onto the middle of one half of a circle. Dab the edges with some water from a small bowl and fold the circle over the Filling to enclose, forming a semicircle. Press firmly along the edges to seal.
5 Pull both ends of the semicircle towards the middle, allowing to overlap slightly. Press the overlapping ends lightly to seal. Set aside and cover with a damp cloth. Repeat until the dough is used up.
6 Place the pot stickers in a skillet and fill $1/4$ of the skillet with water. Cook over high heat until all the water has evaporated and the bottoms of the pot stickers begin to brown, about 1 minute. Flip the pot stickers over to brown the tops, then remove. Serve warm, drizzle with vinegar, and garnish with ginger and spring onion.

Makes 30 pieces   Preparation time: 30 minutes   Cooking time: 15 minutes

balinese beef satays

There are as many recipes for this satay as there are Balinese cooks. The following version is relatively easy to prepare. Dried fermented shrimp paste adds a slightly pungent note while generous quantities of coconut milk give a mild and mellow end result.

2 tablespoons oil
2 cups (500 ml) thick coconut milk
1¼ lbs (600 g) ground beef
18 bamboo skewers (see note)
Lime or lemon wedges, to serve
  (optional)

Spice Paste
2 to 3 red chilies, deseeded and sliced
6 cloves garlic
1 in (2½ cm) fresh ginger root, sliced
1 in (2½ cm) galangal root, sliced
4 candlenuts or macadamia nuts
1 tablespoon ground coriander
4 kaffir lime or *salam* leaves, thinly
  sliced into shreds (optional)
1 teaspoon dried shrimp paste, crumbled
1 teaspoon freshly ground black pepper
2 tablespoons sugar
1 teaspoon salt

1 Grind all the Spice Paste ingredients to a smooth paste in a blender. Heat the oil in a saucepan over medium heat and stir-fry the Spice Paste until fragrant, about 1 minute. Add the coconut milk and simmer for about 8 minutes until it begins to thicken. Set aside to cool.
2 Wet your hands and form the ground beef into small meatballs, using about 1 tablespoon of beef for each one. Marinate the meatballs in the Spice Paste for at least 2 hours in the refrigerator.
3 Thread the meatballs onto bamboo skewers and grill, a few at a time, over medium heat on a charcoal or pan grill until cooked, about 3 minutes on each side.
4 Bring the remaining marinade to a boil in a skillet over medium heat and transfer to a serving bowl. Serve the satays with lime or lemon wedges and the marinade as the dipping sauce.

Note: If grilling the satays over charcoal, soak the bamboo skewers in water for 1 hour before using to keep them from burning.

Makes 18 satays   Preparation time: 30 minutes   Cooking time: 30 minutes

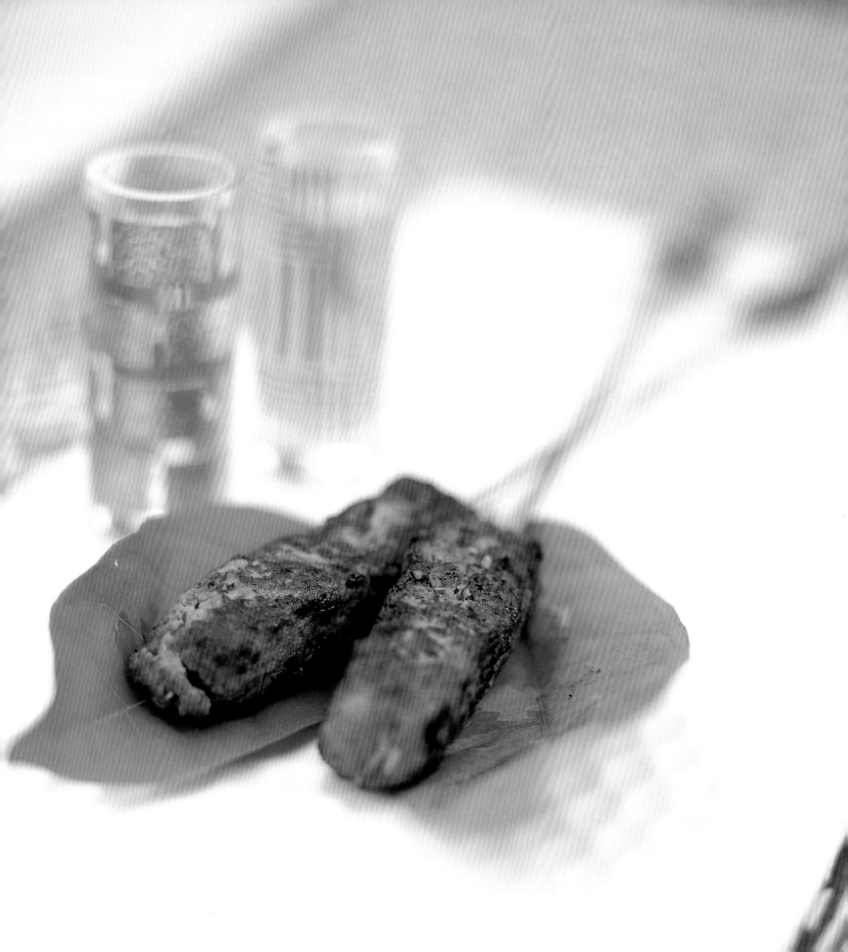

tropical mango sushi

These neat little packages are not complicated to make and are ideal to serve as finger food. Strips of Vietnamese rice paper (normally used for fresh rice paper spring rolls) are used to wrap the sushi in place of the usual *nori* seaweed sheets.

1 large medium-ripe mango (about
    1 lb/ 500 g), peeled and diced
1 shallot, minced
1 small red chili, halved lengthwise,
    deseeded and very thinly sliced
1 teaspoon minced coriander leaves
    (cilantro)
1 teaspoon sugar
1 teaspoon fish sauce
1 tablespoon fresh lime juice
2 teaspoons grated wasabi root
3 dried rice paper wrappers (see note)

Sushi Rice
1 cup (200 g) uncooked short grain
    Japanese rice
$1^1/_2$ cups (350 ml) water
1 sheet *konbu* seaweed, 2 in (5 cm)
    square (optional)
2 tablespoons Japanese rice vinegar
$1^1/_2$ tablespoons sugar
1 tablespoon *mirin*
1 teaspoon salt

1 To make the Sushi Rice, bring the rice, water and *konbu* (if using) to a boil in a saucepan. Discard the *konbu*, then with the saucepan half covered, cook over medium heat for about 5 minutes until all the water has been absorbed. Reduce heat to low and cook covered for a further 10 minutes. Remove from heat and transfer the cooked rice to a mixing bowl to cool. Combine the vinegar, sugar, *mirin* and salt in a bowl and mix until the sugar is dissolved, then add to the cooked rice, tossing gently with a spoon until well combined. Set aside.
2 Combine the diced mango with the shallot, chili, coriander leaves, sugar, fish sauce and lime juice in a bowl. Toss lightly and set aside.
3 Cut the rice paper into 12 small, narrow strips measuring 5 x 1 in (12 x 3 cm) each. Soften the rice paper strips in a bowl of water for 30 seconds and pat dry with paper towels.
4 Wet your palms with a little water and scoop 2 tablespoons of the Sushi Rice to form a small block. Dab a little wasabi on the top of each block of rice and wrap the sides with a strip of the softened rice paper. Continue until the Sushi Rice is used up.
5 Top each sushi block with a tablespoon of the mango mixture and serve at room temperature.

Note: Vietnamese rice paper wrappers are available dried in Asian food stores and are packed in plastic packs of 10 or more round sheets normally measuring about 10 in (25 cm) in diameter.

Makes 12 pieces   Preparation time: 20 minutes   Cooking time: 20 minutes

baked black cod with miso

A paste made from fermented soybeans and various grains, Japanese miso comes in many varieties ranging from salty to sweet. Slightly sweet white miso is called for here but any other type may also be used. Delicate fillets of cod or seabass make an ideal accompaniment to the suave, complex flavors of miso, which is used here to make a delicious marinade.

1 lb (500 g) black cod or seabass, cut
   into thick fillets or steaks
Radish, for garnishing

Miso Marinade
4 tablespoons (60 ml) sake
4 tablespoons (60 ml) *mirin*
4 teaspoons (120 g) white miso paste
$1/2$ teaspoon sugar

1 To make the Miso Marinade, combine all the ingredients in a saucepan and simmer over low heat for about 5 minutes, stirring constantly, until it thickens. Remove pan from heat and set aside to cool.
2 Reserve 2 tablespoons of the Miso Marinade to use as a dipping sauce and place the fish slices in the remaining Miso Marinade. Marinate in the refrigerator at least overnight or 2 nights if possible to allow the marinade to infuse the fish.
3 Preheat the oven to 400°F (200°C). Place the fish slices on a baking sheet and bake in the oven for 5 minutes, turning on the broiler for the last 2 minutes or so to glaze the top of the fish to a golden brown.
4 Brush the top of the fish with the reserved Miso Marinade and garnish with radish. Serve warm with a dipping bowl of the remaining Miso Marinade on the side.

Note: *Mirin* is a sweet sake made by mixing and fermenting steamed glutinous rice with *shoju*. Bottled *mirin* is available in well stocked supermarkets and Japanese supermarkets.

Makes 4 portions or serves 4   Preparation time: 20 minutes + overnight marination   Cooking time: 10 minutes

kashmiri shrimp kebabs with ginger and coriander

Kebabs are served both as a first or main course in India and are even eaten as a snack purchased from street vendors. There are plenty of kebab variations; here, fresh ginger root, green chili and coriander leaves provide an unforgettable combination.

10 oz (300 g) fresh shrimp, peeled, deveined and processed to a coarse paste in a food processor
1 teaspoon ground red pepper
1 teaspoon ground caraway seeds
$1^1/_2$ teaspoons ground coriander
$1^1/_2$ tablespoons grated fresh ginger
1 tablespoon minced green chili
$^1/_2$ teaspoon salt
1 tablespoon minced coriander leaves (cilantro)
12 lemongrass stalks (or stainless steel skewers), washed, outer layers removed and discarded
Lime wedges, to serve

1 Preheat the oven to 400°F (200°C).
2 Combine the processed shrimp, red pepper, caraway, ground coriander, ginger, chili, salt and coriander leaves in a bowl and mix well. Divide the shrimp mixture into 12 equal portions. Wrap each portion around the base of a lemongrass stalk or stainless skewer to obtain 12 kebabs.
3 Place the kebabs on a baking tray and bake in the oven at 400°F (200°C) for 6 minutes. Serve hot with lime wedges.

Makes 12 kebabs   Preparation time: 20 minutes   Cooking time: 6 minutes

baked kangkong wonton rolls with goat cheese

Maximum impact for minimal fuss is guaranteed with these tasty rolls, which are a playful variant on the stuffed pasta theme. Chili-hot sambal with goat cheese, leafy *kangkong* (water spinach) and garlic are the basis of the full-flavored filling and readily-available fresh wonton wrappers provide the wrapping. Use bok choy if *kangkong* is not available.

2 cups (500 ml) water
12 fresh or frozen wonton wrappers
Ice water
1 egg, beaten
1 teaspoon olive oil
1 tablespoon grated parmesan cheese
1 tablespoon chili oil (optional)

Filling
1 tablespoon olive oil
2 cloves garlic, smashed
2 cups (100 g) *kangkong* (see note) or
   bok choy, coarsely chopped
$1/4$ teaspoon salt
1 tablespoon goat cheese
$1/2$ teaspoon freshly ground black
   pepper
1 tablespoon *sambal oelek* (see note)

1 To make the Filling, heat the olive oil in a skillet over medium heat and stir-fry the garlic, *kangkong* (or bok choy) and salt for 1 minute until half cooked. Transfer to a bowl and remove the garlic. Strain or squeeze the *kangkong* to remove the liquid. Return to the bowl and stir in the goat cheese, pepper and *sambal oelek*, mixing well.
2 Preheat the oven to 400°F (200°C).
3 Bring the water to a boil in a pot and quickly blanch each wonton wrapper for 10 seconds to soften. Plunge the wrappers into ice water immediately after blanching to stop further cooking. Drain and set aside.
4 Pat the wonton wrappers dry with paper towels. Spread each wrapper on a flat surface and place 1 tablespoon of the Filling along the edge of the wrapper closest to you. Roll the wonton up tightly and seal the edges with dabs of beaten egg.
5 Lightly grease a baking tray with the olive oil and place the rolls on the tray, sprinkling a little parmesan cheese on top of each roll. Bake in the oven for 10 minutes at 400°F (200°C). When cooked, halve each roll and drizzle with chili oil (if using). Serve warm.

Note: *Kangkong* or water spinach (also known as morning glory) is a leafy green with long, crunchy stems. It is widely available now in Asian food stores. Bok choy makes a good substitute. *Sambal oelek* is the Indonesian version of *sambal belachan* but is sweeter. It is widely available in small jars in Asian food stores and large supermarkets. Any dark sweet chili paste containing dried shrimp, shallots and garlic works well in this recipe.

Makes 24 rolls   Preparation time: 30 minutes   Cooking time: 15 minutes

abalone windmill dumplings

Abalone is an extravagant ingredient, highly valued throughout the Orient for its healing properties, as well as for its unmatched flavor and texture. Serve these eye-catching dumplings at a party buffet where they are sure to be a great conversation piece.

1 cup (125 g) tapioca flour (*tam min fun*) (see note)
1¼ cups (300 ml) boiling water
1 cup (120 g) cornstarch
Napa cabbage leaves, for steaming
Soy sauce or black vinegar, to serve

Filling
7 oz (200 g) fresh shrimp, peeled and deveined, chopped
2 large abalone (7 oz/200 g in total) or 1 can (1 lb/450 g) pacific clams, chopped
½ cup (50 g) diced bamboo shoot
½ cup (50 g) diced carrot
½ cup (5 pieces/100 g) dried bamboo pith, soaked in water until soft, drained and diced
1 teaspoon sesame oil
½ teaspoon sugar
¼ teaspoon salt
¼ teaspoon ground white pepper

1 To make the Filling, combine all the ingredients in a large bowl and mix well. Set aside.
2 To make the dough, combine the tapioca flour and boiling water in a mixing bowl and mix vigorously with a wooden stick or spoon. Add the cornstarch and mix until well blended. Transfer to a floured surface and knead with your hands until a smooth, elastic dough is obtained. Form into a ball and cover with a damp cloth or plastic wrap.
3 Flour your hands, pull out about ½ tablespoon of the dough and form it into a small ball. Repeat until the dough is used up, cover with a damp cloth or plastic wrap and set aside.
4 On a floured surface, make the dumpling wrappers by flattening each ball with your palm, then rolling it out gently with one hand, while rotating it in the opposite direction with the other hand, to form a thin circle approximately 4 in (10 cm) in diameter.
5 Place a wrapper on your palm and spoon ½ tablespoon of the Filling onto the center. Using your fingers, take the edges of the wrapper and fold up to form a three-sided pyramid shaped dumpling. Seal the dumpling by pressing gently along the edges, dabbing your fingers in a little bowl of water to help the seams to bond. Make all the dumplings in this manner.
6 Line the steamer with napa cabbage leaves, place the dumplings on top and steam for about 6 minutes until translucent.
7 Serve with soy sauce or black vinegar.

Note: If tapioca flour is not available, you may use plain flour instead.

Makes 50 dumplings   Preparation time: 45 minutes   Cooking time: 6 minutes

tropical shrimp and fruit salad

A little tart and just vaguely fruity, raw green papaya tastes like a refreshing, summer vegetable. In combination with the sweet, sour and salty flavors of pineapple, mango, lime, sugar and fish sauce, and further enhanced by mint, shrimp and cashews, it makes an unforgettable salad.

4 cups (1 liter) water
1 teaspoon salt
1 teaspoon sugar
12 fresh medium shrimp (about 9 oz/ 250 g)
Ice water
5 tablespoons lime juice
2 tablespoons fish sauce
1 tablespoon sugar
12 mint leaves, thinly sliced
1 cup diced firm mango
1 cup diced green papaya
1 cup diced fresh pineapple
$1/2$ medium onion, sliced into thin strips
2 to 3 red chilies, halved lengthwise, deseeded and sliced into long, thin shreds
12 roasted cashew nuts, finely chopped or pulsed briefly in a blender

1 Bring the water, salt and sugar to a boil in a pot. Add the shrimp and boil uncovered for 2 minutes. Remove and plunge into ice water. Peel and devein the chilled shrimp, then set aside.

2 Combine the lime juice, fish sauce, sugar and mint leaves in a large bowl and stir until the sugar is dissolved. Add the mango, papaya, pineapple, onion and chilies, and toss until well mixed.

3 To assemble, place 2 tablespoons of the fruit mixture in a serving bowl, top with a shrimp and a sprinkling of cashew nuts. Repeat to obtain 12 portions. Serve chilled.

Makes 12 portions   Preparation time: 30 minutes   Cooking time: 5 minutes

beef yakitori with eggplant

Eggplant with beef is a time-honored union, celebrated in many Asian and Mediterranean cuisines. The overnight marination and flash-fast cooking here ensure that the steak is extremely tender and the eggplant, pillow-soft.

10 oz (300 g) beef sirloin (preferably Japanese *kobe* or *wagyu* beef), cubed (see note)
2 teaspoons sesame oil
1 slender Asian eggplant (about 7 oz/200 g), sliced into $1/2$ in (1 cm) sections
Pinch of salt
18 bamboo skewers
$1/2$ tablespoon butter
$1/2$ tablespoon olive oil

Yakitori Marinade
3 tablespoons soy sauce
2 tablespoons black soy sauce
1 tablespoon *ponzu* sauce (see note)
1 tablespoon sugar
1 teaspoon freshly ground black pepper

1 Combine the Yakitori Marinade ingredients in a bowl and stir well until the sugar is dissolved. Marinate the beef in the Yakitori Marinade for at least 4 hours or overnight if possible.
2 Heat the sesame oil in a skillet over high heat, sear the eggplant sections, with a sprinkling of salt, for 30 seconds on each side. Set aside.
3 Thread 1 section of the eggplant, followed by 1 beef cube, then another section of the eggplant on a bamboo skewer. Repeat until all the ingredients are used up.
4 Heat the butter and olive oil in a nonstick skillet over high heat. Sear the skewers on each side for 10 seconds until brown on the outside but still rare inside. Serve hot.

Note: Japanese *kobe* or *wagyu* beef is evenly marbled and melts in your mouth. Well-marbled, high quality beef works best in this recipe. *Ponzu* sauce is a mixture of soy, lemon juice, *mirin,* sake, *konbu* and bonito flakes and is available in small bottles in Asian food stores.

Makes 18 pieces   Preparation time: 20 minutes + overnight marination
Cooking time: 5 minutes

crisp starfruit and asparagus salad

Liberal use of herbs, raw or blanched vegetables, and sour fruits such as the starfruit (carambola) featured in this dish, are hallmarks of Vietnamese-style cookery. Fish sauce, lime and sugar also mark this dish as Vietnamese in it's inspiration as does the overall result, which is light, pretty and fresh-flavored. If starfruit is not available, try this recipe with crisp green apple slices.

3 cups (750 ml) water
2 dried sweet Chinese sausages (*lap cheong*) (see note)
1 starfruit (about 4 oz/125 g) or carambola, trimmed and thinly sliced
2 large or 4 medium asparagus spears (about 4 oz/125 g), thick bottom one third removed and discarded
4 long beans, cut into 2-in (5-cm) lengths
Ice water
1 cup (60 g) bean sprouts, heads and tails removed

Vietnamese Mint Dressing
3 tablespoons fish sauce
2 tablespoons fresh lime juice
2 tablespoons sugar
1 teaspoon Chinese sweet plum powder or plum sauce
10 Vietnamese mint leaves (*rau ram*) or *laksa* leaves (polygonum), sliced (see note)
2 bird's-eye chilies, deseeded and minced (optional)

1 To make the Vietnamese Mint Dressing, combine all the ingredients in a bowl and mix until the sugar dissolves. Set aside.
2 Blanch the sausage over high heat for about 1 minute, then peel off the gelatin skin and slice into matchsticks. Set aside.
3 Lightly blanch the asparagus and long beans for less than 1 minute, then plunge into ice water to cool. Drain in a colander and set aside. Blanch the bean sprouts in the same pot of boiling water for 5 seconds, then cool and drain in the same manner and set aside.
4 Combine the sausage, starfruit slices and the blanched vegetables in a salad bowl. Pour the Vietnamese Mint Dressing over and toss to mix well. Serve cold.

Note: Dried sweet Chinese sausages (*lap cheong*) are sold in Chinese grocery shops and can be seen tied and hanging in bunches or in netting bags. They are finger-sized and bright red in color. Sweet dried salami may be substituted. Vietnamese mint leaves (*rau ram* or *laksa*), also known as polygonum leaves, are widely available in Asian food stores and wet markets. If unavailable, substitute with a mixture of fresh mint, basil and coriander leaves (cilantro).

Makes 10 cocktail portions or serves 4   Preparation time: 15 minutes
Cooking time: 3 minutes

honey glazed baby squids

The sweetness of tender baby squids is enhanced by a little honey, oyster sauce and tomato ketchup in this heavenly dish. A brief glazing turns the squid a beautiful burnished bronze, after which it is ready to be served atop crisp, fried rounds of Shanghainese *man tou* bun.

Oil for deep-frying
10 oz (300 g) fresh baby squids, cleaned
1$^1/_2$ tablespoons honey
2 tablespoons oyster sauce
2 tablespoons tomato ketchup
$^1/_2$ tablespoon black soy sauce
2 teaspoons sugar
$^1/_4$ teaspoon salt
1 teaspoon grated lemon zest
5 sweet buns (*man tou*) or 15 fresh
  baguette slices

1 Deep-fry the baby squids over high heat for 10 minutes, or until very crispy. Remove from heat and drain well on paper towels. Set aside.
2 Combine the honey, oyster sauce, tomato ketchup, black soy sauce, sugar, salt and lemon zest in a skillet and mix well. Place the squids in the sauce mixture and cook over medium heat, stirring constantly, until the squids are well coated.
3 Deep-fry the buns until golden brown. Cut the buns into thirds and top each slice of bun with some baby squids. Drizzle the extra sauce over the squids and serve.

Makes 15 pieces   Preparation time: 25 minutes   Cooking time: 15 minutes

spicy kimchi pancakes with vinegar soy dipping sauce

Kimchi, the fiery-hot cabbage pickles, originates from Korea, where it is practically a national obsession. Stirred into a pancake batter and gently cooked into crisp little fritters, its chili-garlic heat becomes nicely tempered.

$^3/_4$ cup (120 g) flour
1 egg
1 cup (250 ml) water
1 green and 1 red chili, deseeded and
  sliced lengthwise into fine shreds
1 spring onion, minced
1 cup (100 g) diced cabbage kimchi
1 tablespoon white sesame seeds, lightly
  dry-roasted in a pan until fragrant
3 tablespoons olive oil
$^1/_2$ cup (25 g) fresh beansprouts, to
  serve (optional)

Vinegar Soy Dipping Sauce
2 teaspoons rice vinegar
6 teaspoons soy sauce
3 teaspoons sesame seeds
2 teaspoons dry chili flakes

1 Make the Vinegar Soy Dipping Sauce first by combining all the ingredients in a serving bowl and mixing well. Set aside.
2 Place the flour in a bowl and make a well in the center. Add the egg and whisk well, gradually adding the water. Stir in the red and green chilies, spring onion, kimchi and sesame seeds, mixing well.
3 Heat $^1/_2$ tablespoon of the olive oil in a nonstick skillet over medium-high heat. Make small pancakes by pouring 1 tablespoon of the batter onto the skillet. Gently pan-fry each pancake for 2 minutes on each side until light brown, pressing the pancake flat after turning. Repeat until the mixture is used up. Serve on a bed of raw beansprouts (if using), with a bowl of the Vinegar Soy Dipping Sauce on the side.

Makes 12 pieces   Preparation time: 20 minutes   Cooking time: 10 minutes

smoked turkey and green mango salad

Like green papaya, green mango makes for cooling summer salads, lending them a slightly fruity note. Smoked turkey and freshly roasted cashews work fabulously here with the essentially simple line-up of flavors—lime, chili, shallots and coriander.

1 unripe mango (about 5 oz/150 g), peeled and sliced into thin shreds to yield $^1/_2$ cup
1 red chili, deseeded and minced
1 bird's-eye chili, minced
1 tablespoon minced spring onion
2 tablespoons minced shallots
1 tablespoon minced coriander leaves (cilantro)
3 oz (100 g) smoked turkey, diced to yield $^1/_2$ cup
1 teaspoon lime juice
2 tablespoons mayonnaise
$^1/_2$ cup (70 g) raw cashew nuts
Few drops of olive oil
20 fried shrimp crackers (*krupuk*) or pappadams or other crisp wafers, to serve

1 Combine the shredded mango, red chili, bird's-eye chili, spring onion, shallots, coriander leaves, turkey, lime juice and mayonnaise in a mixing bowl, and toss to mix well.
2 Dry-fry the cashew nuts in a skillet over low heat until golden brown, about 5 minutes. Add a few drops of the olive oil to coat the nuts and make them shiny. Finely chop the cashew nuts or pulse briefly to a coarse powder with a blender. Remove and set aside to cool.
3 Add the chopped or ground cashew nuts to the salad mixture and toss to combine well. If the salad mixture is too dry, add more lime juice. Serve with shrimp crackers or pappadams or other crisp wafers.

Makes 20 cocktail portions or serves 4 as an appetizer
Preparation time: 20 minutes   Cooking time: 5 minutes

fragrant khandvi rolls

Chickpea flour, also called garbanzo flour, has a nutty, earthy flavor that is the perfect foil for rich spicing and coconut. Serve these wonderfully fragrant rolls warm with drinks.

2 tablespoons oil
25 to 30 fresh curry leaves or basil leaves, stems removed
2 teaspoons mustard seeds
1 teaspoon ground turmeric
1 teaspoon ground red pepper
1 teaspoon salt
1 cup (200 g) chickpea flour
3 tablespoons plain yoghurt
1 tablespoon oil
2 cups (500 ml) water
2 to 3 tablespoons freshly grated coconut
1 tablespoon minced coriander leaves (cilantro)

1 Heat the oil in a skillet and pan-fry the curry leaves or basil leaves for 30 seconds until they change color and become crispy. Remove the leaves and set aside. Pan-fry the mustard seeds in the same oil for 30 seconds until the seeds pop. Remove from the pan and set aside.

2 Combine the turmeric, red pepper, salt and chickpea flour in a bowl. Add the yoghurt and oil and mix well. Add the water gradually and stir gently until smooth. Pour the batter into a skillet and cook over medium heat for 7 minutes, stirring constantly until it becomes very thick.

3 Quickly transfer the mixture to a large baking tray or cookie sheet and spread it very thinly with a spatula into a flat rectangular sheet about $1/8$ in (3 mm) thick. Trim the edges with a knife to straighten. Cut the sheet into half lengthwise and sprinkle both halves with the grated coconut and minced coriander leaves. Roll each of the halves up tightly into a log, placing the seam side down. Cut the logs into bite-sized rolls, place them on a serving platter on individual plates, sprinkle with the fried mustard seeds and curry or basil leaves.

Makes 24 pieces   Preparation time: 25 minutes   Cooking time: 8 minutes

spicy fish otah morsels

Otah-otah is a fragrant seafood delicacy from the culinary repertoire of the Straits or Nonya Chinese of Malaysia and Singapore. Long coconut palm leaves are filled with a fragrant spice paste and chunks of fish or shrimp, then roasted over an open flame. Once pounded laboriously by hand, these days food processors make quick work of preparing the spice mixture. Palm leaves are the traditional wrapping but paper bark makes an interesting alternative; if neither is available, simply bake the mixture in lightly greased muffin pans and slice into serving portions.

7 oz (200 g) fresh white fish fillets, thinly sliced
1 teaspoon salt
$1/2$ teaspoon ground white pepper
2 tablespoons sugar
1 teaspoon minced *laksa* leaves or Vietnamese mint leaves (see note)
$3^1/_2$ tablespoons coconut cream
1 sheet paper bark

Spice Paste
$2^1/_2$ in (6 cm) galangal root, peeled and sliced
3 stalks lemongrass, thick bottom third only, outer layers discarded, inner part sliced
10 shallots
3 teaspoons ground turmeric
5 red chilies, deseeded and sliced

1 Preheat the oven to 300°F (150°C).
2 To make the Spice Paste, grind all the ingredients to a smooth paste in a blender.
3 Combine the Spice Paste with the fish, salt, pepper, sugar, *laksa* leaves or Vietnamese mint leaves and coconut cream in a bowl and mix well. Spoon the fish mixture onto a sheet of paper bark measuring 10 x 4 in (25 x 10 cm) and roll the sheet into a log measuring 10 in (25 cm) in length, $1^1/_4$ in (3 cm) in diameter. Place the log on a baking tray and bake for 10 minutes. When cooked, cut the log into bite-sized disks and serve hot. Alternatively, the fish mixture may be cooked in a heat-proof baking dish covered with aluminum foil and then sliced into brownie-sized serving portions.

Note: *Laksa* leaves or Vietnamese mint leaves (*rau ram*) are available fresh in Asian grocery stores (they are also known as polygonum leaves). If you cannot find them, substitute Asian or sweet basil.

Serves 4 to 6   Preparation time: 25 minutes   Cooking time: 10 minutes

summer green tea noodles with mussels

The clean flavors of soy sauce and bonito join forces with slippery soba noodles, fresh mussels and the pleasant fragrance of celery leaves to create a dish that's ideal to serve on a hot day. The summery bite of black olives and sundried tomatoes adds another bright element to this lovely, uncomplicated dish.

16 fresh mussels (about 1 lb/500 g) or 12 fresh medium shrimp (about 9 oz/250 g)
7 oz (200 g) dried green tea soba noodles
Ice water
2 tablespoons oyster sauce
2 tablespoons soy sauce
2 tablespoons fine bonito flakes
16 pitted black olives, whole or halved
$1/2$ cup (40 g) sundried tomatoes, sliced
4 tablespoons minced celery leaves, to garnish

1 Scrub the mussels under running water to remove sand and dirt. Blanch the mussels for about 2 minutes until they are all open. Drain and set aside to cool. Once cool, remove mussels from their shells and discard the shells. If using shrimp instead of mussels, blanch them for 2 minutes until they turn pink. Drain and shell the shrimp. Discard the shells and set the shrimp aside to cool.

2 Boil the green tea soba noodles for 5 to 7 minutes until soft. Remove and plunge the noodles in ice water to cool. Drain and set aside.

3 Combine the oyster sauce, soy sauce and bonito flakes in a saucepan and stir to mix well. Bring the sauce mixture to a boil, then simmer for about 5 seconds, remove from heat and set aside to cool.

4 Place the noodles, mussels or shrimp, black olives and sundried tomatoes in a serving bowl. Pour the sauce and gently toss to mix thoroughly. Serve cold, garnished with the celery leaves.

Note: Green tea soba noodles are sold in plastic packets in Asian food stores and look like thin linguine (though usually much shorter). Bonito flakes are the shavings of dried, cured tuna fish and have a smoky taste almost like fine ham or air-dried beef. They are available in small packets in coarse or fine flakes (the coarse ones are used for making *dashi* stock).

Makes 8 servings   Preparation time: 20 minutes   Cooking time: 15 minutes

sesame crusted tuna balls with ginger

Little explosions of flavor, these quickly made tuna balls are a sophisticated accompaniment to a pre-dinner aperitif. Ginger and chives balance the mild meatiness of tuna, and sesame seeds give a dramatic finish.

9 oz (250 g) fresh tuna, minced
2 teaspoons minced red chili
2 tablespoons minced chives
1 teaspoon salt
$1/_2$ teaspoon freshly ground black pepper
2 teaspoons sesame oil
$1^1/_2$ tablespoons grated fesh ginger
4 tablespoons sesame seeds (if possible, a mixture of black and white)
Oil for deep-frying
15 toothpicks

1 Combine the minced tuna with the chili, chives, salt, pepper, sesame oil and ginger in a bowl and mix well.
2 Place the sesame seeds in a plate. Wet your hands, scoop 1 tablespoon of the tuna mixture and roll it into a ball. Roll the tuna ball in the sesame seeds until well coated on all sides. Repeat until the tuna mixture is used up.
3 Deep-fry the tuna balls over high heat for 1 minute, turning constantly. Serve hot with toothpicks.

Makes 15 tuna balls   Preparation time: 15 minutes   Cooking time: 3 minutes

fresh salmon salad rolls

Inspiration for these gorgeously delicate rolls comes from *Yu Sheng*, a raw fish salad eaten by Singaporeans during the Lunar New Year celebrations. Light, fresh and nutty flavors come prettily bundled in rice paper wrappers, with little dabs of tasty tobiko fish roe lending an elegant finishing touch.

6 dried rice paper wrappers (see note)
10 oz (300 g) fresh salmon fillets
Wasabi tobiko or salmon roe (see note), to garnish
Spring onions, to garnish

Filling
$1/2$ cup carrot, cut into fine shreds
$1/2$ cup daikon, cut into fine shreds
2 tablespoons minced coriander leaves (cilantro)
3 tablespoons sweet plum sauce
1 tablespoon sesame oil
2 tablespoons fish sauce
3 tablespoons crushed unsalted roasted peanuts
1 tablespoon sesame seeds, dry-roasted in a skillet until brown
3 teaspoons lime juice

1 To make the Filling, combine all the ingredients in a bowl and toss to mix well. Set aside.

2 Quarter each dried rice paper wrapper and trim the sides to form 4 squares. Briefly soak the squares in water to soften, then pat dry with paper towels.

3 Cut the salmon fillets into 24 very thin slices. Place a slice of salmon and 1 tablespoon of the Filling onto each rice paper square and roll up tightly into a bite-sized piece. Garnish with tobiko or salmon roe and spring onions, and serve chilled.

Note: Dried rice paper wrappers are sold in Asian food stores in plastic packets containing 10 or more wrappers. They are round and white, about 10 in (25 cm) in diameter. Pale green wasabi tobiko roe is tobiko roe that has been flavored with wasabi. Fresh wasabi tobiko roe can be purchased in packets in Japanese supermarkets.

Makes 24 rolls   Preparation time: 25 minutes

crispy lobster and scallop nests with yuzu garlic sauce

Kadaifa pastry is a unique, Middle-Eastern ingredient made up of fine dough strands that are cooked to form crunchy, golden threads. Here they form "nests" for a delicious shrimp and lobster or scallop fillings; the contrasting textures, and lovely presentation, make this a very special dish.

Oil for deep-frying
Mint leaves, to garnish
Sweet black soy sauce, for dipping
  (optional)

Lobster Nests
1 small lobster or 8 small crayfish
3 oz (100 g) fresh shrimp, peeled,
  deveined and ground to a paste in a
  food processor
$1/_4$ teaspoon salt
$1/_4$ teaspoon ground white pepper
1 packet (120 g) *kadaifa* pastry (see note)

Scallop Nests
1 egg
4 tablespoons cornstarch
2 tablespoons water
12 fresh large scallops, shelled
12 slices (15 g) pickled ginger
1 packet (120 g) *kadaifa* pastry (see
  note)

Yuzu Garlic Sauce
1 teaspoon sesame oil
2 tablespoons soy sauce
$3^1/_2$ tablespoons *yuzu* or a mixture of
  mandarin orange and lemon juice
1 teaspoon ground white pepper
3 cloves garlic, minced

1 First make the Yuzu Garlic Sauce by combining all the ingredients in a bowl and mixing well. Set aside.

2 To make the Lobster Nests, poach the lobster until pink, about 3 minutes. Remove and set aside. When cool, shell the lobster and cut into 8 long pieces. If using crayfish, poach and shell. Season the shrimp paste with the salt and pepper in a bowl, and mix well. Wet your hands and wrap each piece of lobster or crayfish in 1 tablespoon of the shrimp paste and form into a roll. Coil the *kadaifa* pastry around the roll once lengthwise, then crosswise repeatedly until the roll is completely wrapped with the pastry. Repeat the process until all the ingredients are used up.

3 To make the Scallop Nests, whisk the egg until light and fluffy, add the cornstarch and water and mix until well blended. Make a slit in the side of each scallop and insert a piece of pickled ginger. Dip each scallop in the cornstarch batter, then roll the scallop in the *kadaifa* pastry to coat.

4 Deep-fry the lobster rolls in hot oil for about 2 minutes each and the coated scallops for about 4 minutes each, until golden brown. Remove and drain on paper towels.

5 Cut each lobster roll in half. Arrange the Lobster and Scallop Nests on a platter. Garnish with mint leaves and serve with Yuzu Garlic Sauce or sweet black soy sauce.

Note: If *kadaifa* pastry is not available, you may use the filo pastry instead. Cut the filo pastry into thin strands and coil around the lobster rolls or coat the scallops in the same manner.

Makes 16 lobster and 12 scallop pieces   Preparation time: 40 minutes
Cooking time: 20 minutes

shrimp and kailan caillettes with horseradish

Caillette is a small, slightly flattened French sausage made from pork, liver, garlic and herbs wrapped in caul fat. Try and get caul fat for this recipe (ask your butcher). It not only provides the wrapping for the caillettes but melts into them as they cook, giving them the most luscious basting imaginable. Filo pastry is a delicious substitute, though, and spinach can stand in for the *kailan*, the leafy Chinese green used here.

4 oz (100 g) caul fat or 4 sheets filo pastry (see note)
1 teaspoon sesame oil

Filling
1 tablespoon olive oil
1 cup (45 g) minced *kailan* or spinach-leaves
Pinch of salt
5 fresh medium shrimp (about 3 oz/100 g), peeled and deveined
3 tablespoons grated fresh horseradish or 2$^1/_2$ tablespoons bottled horseradish
1 teaspoon thinly sliced sundried tomatoes
1 teaspoon chopped pitted black olives
3 tablespoons (40 g) fresh goat cheese
1 egg
$^1/_2$ tablespoon dried shrimp, soaked in water to soften and coarsely ground with a blender
2 tablespoons breadcrumbs

1 To make the Filling, heat $^1/_2$ tablespoon of the olive oil in a skillet over medium heat and stir-fry the *kailan* or spinach leaves with the salt for 2 minutes. Remove and set aside. Heat the remaining olive oil in the skillet and briefly sear the shrimp over high heat, about 15 seconds on each side. Remove and dice into small pieces. Mix the *kailan* or spinach, shrimp pieces and all the other ingredients until well combined in a large bowl. Set aside.

2 Spread out a sheet of the caul fat on a large chopping board and trim to obtain an 8-in (20-cm) square. Place 1 tablespoon of the Filling in the center of the square and fold to enclose the Filling, forming a small package. Wrap all the Filling with caul fat in this manner.

3 Heat the sesame oil in a skillet and pan-fry the packages over medium heat until golden brown, about 2 minutes on each side.

Note: If using filo pastry in place of the caul fat, trim each sheet (20 x 11 in/50 x 28 cm) into 9 x 3-in (23 x 8-cm) rectangles. Place 1 tablespoon of the Filling on each rectangle and fold into a triangular samosa shape.

Makes 10 pieces   Preparation time: 30 minutes   Cooking time: 10 minutes

mussels steamed in fragrant coconut cream

Few things are more alluring or more effortless to produce than steamed mussels. When their briny flavors are teamed with rich coconut cream, lemongrass, lime zest and fragrant Thai curry spices, they become something utterly sublime.

18 fresh green mussels (about 1 lb/500 g)
Ice water
2 stalks lemongrass, thick bottom third
   only, outer layers removed, inner part
   bruised and halved lengthwise
1 tablespoon minced coriander leaves
   (cilantro)
2 teaspoons grated kaffir lime zest (see
   note)
1 spring onion, minced
2 to 3 red chilies, deseeded and minced
3 teaspoons Thai curry paste (see note)
$1/_2$ cup (125 ml) coconut cream
$1/_2$ cup (125 ml) water
2 tablespoons fish sauce
$1/_2$ teaspoon salt

1 Scrub the mussels under running water to remove sand and dirt. Blanch the mussels for about 2 minutes or until they are all open. Remove and plunge in ice water. Drain and set aside.

2 Bring all the other ingredients to a boil in a saucepan over medium heat. After about 3 minutes, add the cooked mussels, cover and simmer for 3 more minutes. Remove and serve hot.

Note: Thai curry paste is available in jars and in packets in Asian food stores. There are different types, look for seafood curry paste if available. But any type can be used. Kaffir limes are fragrant Asian limes with a thick, knobbly skin. The grated rind has a wonderful perfume—if not available, use normal lime zest.

Serves 4   Preparation time: 20 minutes   Cooking time: 8 minutes

fresh pomelo salad with dried shrimp

Sweeter and somewhat drier than pink grapefruit, the pomelo is a large citrus fruit native to Southeast Asia. The slightly acidic flesh stands up well when combined with assertive flavors such as chilli, fish sauce and lime—be sure to remove all the thick pith before pulling the sections apart with your fingers and peeling them to reveal the pulp. Grapefruit makes a suitable substitute. Since it is more bitter and sour than pomelo, more sugar should be added.

3 tablespoons dried shrimp
1 tablespoon olive oil
3 cloves garlic, minced
1 to 2 red chilies, very thinly sliced
1 shallot, minced
2 teaspoons fish sauce
2 tablespoons lime juice
2 teaspoons sugar (double if using grapefruit rather than pomelo)
$1/2$ teaspoon salt
$1/4$ teaspoon ground white pepper
3 tablespoons water
1 pomelo (see note) or 2 grapefruits, peeled and shredded to yield 2 cups pulp
3 tablespoons roasted unsalted peanuts, coarsely ground
20 to 30 fresh mint leaves, to garnish

1 Rinse the dried shrimp well, peeling off any remaining shells. Drain and fry the shrimp pieces in a nonstick skillet over low heat for about 5 minutes. Grind the shrimp to a coarse powder in a blender. Set aside.
2 Heat the olive oil in a skillet over medium heat and sauté the garlic until golden brown and fragrant, about 1 minute. Add the chilies, shallot, fish sauce, lime juice, sugar, salt, pepper and water, and simmer for about 5 minutes. Remove from heat. Place the pomelo or grapefruits in a serving bowl, add the sauce, dried shrimp and peanuts, and toss well to mix.
3 Serve chilled, garnished with mint leaves.

Note: Pomelos are sold fresh in Asian food stores. They are very large and round, with a pointed tip and a smooth, green skin that is similar to a grapefruit.

Makes 30 cocktail portions or serves 4 as an appetizer
Preparation time: 30 minutes   Cooking time: 15 minutes

green tea noodle shrimp tempura

A delicate tangle of subtly-flavored green tea noodles and tender shrimp make for a spectacular tempura. Ice in the batter is the secret to a very light and crisp coating—be sure to serve these as quickly after cooking as possible while they are still hot and crunchy.

2 oz (60 g) green tea soba noodles (see note)
Ice water
$1/2$ cup (75 g) flour
1 egg yolk
$1/3$ cup (80 ml) water
$1/3$ cup ice cubes
10 large fresh shrimp or prawns (about 12 oz/350 g), peeled and deveined
1 tablespoon cornstarch
Oil for deep-frying
Sweet garlic chili sauce, for dipping

Sundried Tomato Dip
2 tablespoons minced sundried tomatoes
$1/2$ cup (125 g) sour cream
2 tablespoons garlic chives
2 tablespoons Tabasco sauce

1 To make the Sundried Tomato Dip, mix all the ingredients in a bowl until well combined. Transfer to a serving bowl and refrigerate for 3 hours before serving.
2 Boil the green tea soba noodles for 5 to 7 minutes until soft. Remove and plunge the noodles in ice water to cool. Drain and set aside.
3 Combine the flour, egg yolk and water in a mixing bowl, and whisk to a smooth batter. Add ice cubes and whisk until well blended.
4 Lightly coat a shrimp or prawn with the cornstarch. Dip a few green tea soba noodles in the batter, then remove and wrap the shrimp or prawn in the coated noodles. Repeat with the rest of the shrimp or prawns.
5 Heat the oil in a wok until very hot. Gently lower the shrimp or prawns wrapped with noodles, a few at a time, into the hot oil and deep-fry for about 2 minutes until golden brown and crispy. Remove and drain on paper towels. Serve hot with sweet garlic chili sauce and a bowl of Sundried Tomato Dip on the side.

Note: Japanese green tea soba noodles are sold in packets and look like short, green linguine. Regular, unflavored soba noodles (which are made from buckwheat) may also be used.

Makes 10   Preparation time: 20 minutes   Cooking time: 10 minutes

saffron sushi rice with clams and sausage

Rice is important to the cooking of both Japan and Spain, and here, cultural lines blur in the creation of these tasty rice balls. Saffron, pimentos, chorizo and green peas are characteristically Spanish ingredients, while sushi rice and mild rice vinegar are staples from Japan.

$1/3$ cup (50 g) finely diced cooked chorizo sausage or salami
$1/2$ teaspoon salt
$1/4$ teaspoon freshly ground black pepper
9 pieces grilled red pimentos (see note), each trimmed to 4 rectangular pieces
Horseradish sprouts or baby mustard seed sprouts, to garnish
35 cooked baby clams, to garnish

Green Pea Purée
1 cup (200 g) fresh or frozen green peas
$1^1/2$ teaspoons salt
4 cups (1 liter) water
1 tablespoon olive oil

Red Bell Pepper Sauce
1 red bell pepper (about 3 oz/100 g), deseeded, white pulp removed, sliced
2 bird's-eye chilies, chopped
2 shallots, sliced
1 tablespoon rice vinegar
2 tablespoons sake
2 tablespoons chicken stock or $1/4$ teaspoon chicken stock powder dissolved in 2 tablespoons hot water
1 tablespoon sugar

Saffron Sushi Rice
$1^1/2$ cups (10 oz/300 g) uncooked short grain Japanese rice
$1/2$ teaspoon saffron powder or strands
$1^1/4$ cups (300 ml) water
2 tablespoons (30 ml) rice vinegar

1 To make the Green Pea Purée, boil the green peas, 1 teaspoon salt and water in a saucepan over high heat for 5 minutes. Remove the green peas and reserve the water. In a blender, purée the green peas with $1/2$ cup (125 ml) of the water it was boiled in. Add the remaining salt and olive oil, and blender to a smooth purée. Set aside.

2 To make the Red Bell Pepper Sauce, pulse the pepper, chilies, shallots, rice vinegar, sake and chicken stock several times to chop finely in a blender. Transfer to a saucepan, add the sugar and simmer over medium heat for about 5 minutes, stirring constantly, until thickened. Remove from heat and transfer to a serving bowl. Set aside.

3 To make the Saffron Sushi Rice, bring the rice, saffron and water to a boil over high heat in a saucepan. Reduce heat to low and cook until all the water has evaporated, 10 to 15 minutes. When the rice is cooked, transfer to a large bowl and set aside to cool. Alternatively, you may cook the rice in an electric rice cooker. Pour the rice vinegar over the cooked rice and mix to combine. Set aside to cool.

4 Add the chorizo sausage or salami, salt and black pepper to the Saffron Sushi Rice and mix thoroughly. Wet your hands and spoon 1 tablespoon of rice onto your palm. Squeeze and shape the rice into a ball. Repeat, wetting your hands each time, until the rice is used up.

5 To assemble, top each rice ball with a slice of red pimentos, horseradish sprouts or baby mustard seed sprouts and a cooked clam. Serve with Green Pea Purée or Red Bell Pepper Sauce.

Note: Grilled red pimentos are available in small jars or cans.

Makes 35 rice balls   Preparation time: 45 minutes   Cooking time: 35 minutes

har kow shrimp focaccia buns

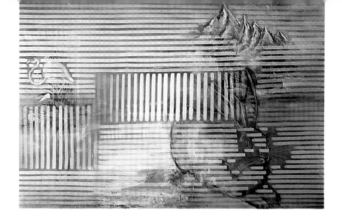

Har Kow is a delicate steamed dumpling that often appears on dim sum trolleys. Focaccia dough, enriched with butter then wrapped around the classic shrimp and bamboo shoot *har kow* filling, makes a delicious savory bun and is an ingenious spin on this Cantonese classic.

$1/2$ cup (160 g) unsalted butter, softened
Flour, for dusting the dough
10 oz (300 g) fresh medium shrimp, peeled and deveined, cut into pieces
Canned or cooked fresh bamboo shoots, scalded in hot water, drained and then diced to yield 1 cup (about 100 g)
1 dried sweet Chinese sausage (*lap cheong*), diced to obtain 3 tablespoons
$1/2$ teaspoon sugar
$1/2$ teaspoon salt
$1/2$ teaspoon freshly ground black pepper
1 egg, beaten

Focaccia Dough
$1/4$ tablespoon instant yeast granules
2 cups (300 g) flour
2 tablespoons softened butter
2 tablespoons olive oil
$1/2$ cup (125 ml) ice water
1 tablespoon salt

1 To make the Focaccia Dough, dissolve the yeast granules in 2 tablespoons of warm water and set aside. Mix the flour, butter and olive oil using a mixer at low speed. After about 5 minutes, add the dissolved yeast. Continue mixing for another 5 minutes, adding the ice water gradually. Mix for a further 10 minutes until a smooth dough is formed. Transfer the dough to a bowl and refrigerate for at least 1 hour.
2 Fold a sheet of wax paper in half and place the butter in between, flattening the butter in the wax paper with your hand into a 7-in (18-cm) square. Chill the butter in the refrigerator until hard.
3 Flour your hands and roll the chilled Focaccia Dough on a lightly floured surface into a large 8 x 15-in (20 x 37-cm) rectangle. Fold the rectangle in half, then remove the chilled butter from the wax paper and place it in between the dough. Press the edges down to seal the butter in and roll the dough out again to lengthen it. Fold one end of the dough to the middle, then fold the other end over it. Roll the dough out again, dusting the surface with flour as necessary. Repeat this rolling process 3 times, resting the dough for 10 minutes each time. Place the dough on a tray, cover with plastic wrap and chill for 2 hours.
4 To make the filling, combine the shrimp pieces, bamboo shoots, sausage, sugar, salt and black pepper in a bowl and mix until well blended. Set aside.
5 Preheat the oven to 400°F (200°C).
6 Remove the dough from the refrigerator and roll into $1/10$ in (2 mm) thick. Cut twenty-four 6-inch (15-cm) circles with a cookie cutter. Place $1^{1}/_{2}$ teaspoons of the filling on each circle, fold the edges and seal into a small stuffed bun. Place the buns on an ovenproof tray, brush the tops with egg and bake in the oven at 400°F (200°C) for 15 minutes. Serve warm.

Makes 24 buns   Preparation time: 1 hour + $2^{1}/_{2}$ hours chilling
Cooking time: 15 minutes

asparagus crab salad with ginger cream

Crisp, thin flatbreads and crackers—Indian pappadams, Indonesian *krupuk* and Vietnamese or Japanese rice and sesame seed crackers—all make the perfect vehicle for this divine crab salad; alternatively, serve it neatly on small spoons or appetizer plates.

9 oz (250 g) cauliflower
4 oz (125 g) fresh asparagus, tender upper part of spears only
$^1/_2$ cup (125 ml) chicken stock or $^1/_2$ chicken stock cube dissolved in $^1/_2$ cup (125 ml) hot water
$^1/_2$ cup (125 ml) cream
1 in ($2^1/_2$ cm) fresh ginger root, thinly sliced
1 teaspoon salt
1 teaspoon ground white pepper
1 medium tomato, blanched, peeled and deseeded, flesh diced
2 tablespoons minced chives
$^1/_2$ tablespoon finely grated lemon zest
1 cup (5 oz/150 g) cooked crabmeat
1 teaspoon olive oil
1 teaspoon sherry vinegar or white wine vinegar
1 sprig coriander leaves (cilantro), to garnish

1 Remove the tender florets of the cauliflower, break them into tiny pieces and set aside for later use (should yield around $1^1/_2$ cups/4 oz of tiny florets). Slice the remaining cauliflower stems into small pieces. Slice the tender upper part of the asparagus spears into small pieces.
2 Place the asparagus and cauliflower pieces into a saucepan with the chicken stock, cream, ginger and $^1/_2$ of the salt and pepper, and bring to a boil over high heat for about 5 minutes. Remove from the heat, allow to cool slightly and purée in a blender until smooth. Place in the refrigerator to chill for 20 minutes.
3 Combine the reserved cauliflower florets with the diced tomato, minced chives and half of the lemon zest in a bowl and mix well. Season with the remaining salt and pepper. Stir in the crabmeat and set aside for 1 minute, then add the olive oil and sherry vinegar, and mix well.
4 When the cauliflower purée is well chilled, add the crabmeat mixture and toss well to combine. Serve chilled, garnished with coriander leaves.

Makes 10 cocktail portions or serves 4   Preparation time: 30 minutes
Cooking time: 10 minutes

tender punjabi chicken kebabs with mint sauce

The Punjab lies in the mountainous northwest of India, on the frontier with Kashmir and Pakistan. A farming region, its cuisine is rich in dairy products—this version of a northern Indian kebab is lighter than those eaten on the subcontinent, being made with chicken instead of lamb and oven-baked instead of fried.

10 oz (300 g) ground chicken or turkey
$^1/_4$ teaspoon ground cumin
$^1/_2$ teaspoon salt
$^1/_2$ teaspoon ground turmeric
$^1/_2$ teaspoon ground cardamom
$^1/_4$ teaspoon ground mace
$^1/_2$ teaspoon minced fresh ginger root
$^1/_2$ teaspoon minced red chili
1 tablespoon minced coriander leaves
  (cilantro)
3 tablespoons finely diced bell peppers
  (if possible, a combination of red,
  green and yellow)
1 tablespoon minced chives or spring
  onions or coriander leaves (cilantro)
6 bamboo skewers
2 teaspoons sesame seeds (preferably a
  mixture of black and white)
Lime wedges, to serve

Mint Sauce
$^1/_2$ cup (125 ml) plain yogurt
4 sprigs mint
1 teaspoon sugar
1 teaspoon salt
$^1/_4$ teaspoon cayenne pepper

1 To make the Mint Sauce, purée all the ingredients in a blender and transfer to a serving bowl. This makes about $^3/_4$ cup of sauce.
2 Preheat the oven to 400°F (200°C).
3 Combine all the ingredients except the sesame seeds in a bowl and mix until well blended. Divide the mixture into 6 portions. Wet your hands, shape each portion into a ball and skewer on a bamboo skewer. Repeat with the remaining portions to obtain 6 kebabs. Set aside.
4 Place the sesame seeds on a plate and roll the kebabs in the sesame seeds to coat on all sides. Bake the kebabs in the oven at 400°F (200°C) for 8 minutes. Remove and discard the bamboo skewers, cut each kebab into segments and serve hot with lime wedges and Mint Sauce.

Note: If preferred, you may make the colorful kebabs as shown in the photos by separating the red, green and yellow bell peppers and mixing with the other ingredients to make red, green and yellow kebabs. Coat these kebabs separately with different colored sesame seeds before baking.

Makes 6 kebabs   Preparation time: 25 minutes   Cooking time: 8 minutes

crisp asparagus rolls with cheese and xo sauce

Perfect pass-around finger fare, these asparagus rolls rely on spicy XO sauce for their punchy tang and filo pastry for their crispness. Instead of the expected baking, here the filo is cooked by careful pan-frying in olive oil.

16 large asparagus spears (about 1 lb/500 g)
6 cups (1$^1/_2$ liters) water with 1 tablespoon of salt
Ice water
2 to 3 sheets filo pastry (20 x 11 in/50 x 28 cm each), for wrapping
6 tablespoons (40 g) grated parmesan cheese
4 teaspoons XO sauce
$^1/_2$ cup (125 ml) melted butter
4 tablespoons olive oil

Step-by-step photos and instructions for this recipe are provided on page 112.

1 Cut off the bottom one-third of the asparagus spears and discard. Blanch the asparagus for 3 minutes in a boiling pot of salted water, drain and quickly plunge the spears into ice water to cool.

2 Cut the filo pastry sheets into rectangular strips whose width matches $^2/_3$ the height of the asparagus spears. Place the grated cheese and the asparagus spears on a large plate, then move the plate to and fro to roll the asparagus in the cheese until well coated.

3 Place each asparagus spear on a filo strip, close to one end. Add $^1/_4$ teaspoon of the XO sauce and wrap the filo strip around the spear 3 to 4 times. Seal the edges with a dab of butter. Repeat the process with the other asparagus spears.

4 Heat the olive oil in a skillet over medium-high heat and pan-fry the asparagus rolls on all sides, placing the sealed edge face down first, until the filo pastry turns golden brown. Serve hot on a platter.

Makes 16 pieces   Preparation time: 20 minutes   Cooking time: 10 minutes

steamed dim sum chicken buns

Steaming yields extraordinarily tender, white buns—this one is typical of those found in Southern Chinese snacks and *dim sum* cookery. Ginger gives an unmistakable lift to the chicken filling; plenty of hot Chinese tea is the perfect accompaniment to the buns.

Dough
2 cups *pau* flour (see note)
$1/3$ cup (70 g) sugar
$1^1/_2$ tablespoons baking powder
$1/_2$ cup (125 ml) water
$1/_2$ tablespoon lard or shortening
Baking paper

Filling
10 oz (300 g) boneless chicken thighs, diced
8 dried Chinese mushrooms, soaked in water until soft, stems removed and discarded, caps diced
$1^1/_2$ cups (150 g) diced bamboo shoots
2 spring onions, minced
1 tablespoon minced fresh ginger root
1 teaspoon salt
$1^1/_2$ teaspoons sugar
$1^1/_2$ teaspoons cornstarch
1 teaspoon sesame oil
$1^1/_2$ teaspoons ground white pepper
$1/_2$ teaspoon chicken stock powder
$1/_2$ teaspoon vegetable oil

Step-by-step photos and instructions for this recipe are provided on page 112.

1 To make the Dough, mix all the ingredients together with a mixer to form a smooth dough, about 5 minutes. Remove and knead on a lightly floured surface to remove all the air bubbles. Cover the dough with a cloth and set aside to rest for $1/_2$ an hour.

2 To make the Filling, combine all the ingredients in a large bowl and mix well. Form into a ball and refrigerate for $1/_2$ an hour.

3 Cut 20 square pieces of baking paper, each about 2 in (5 cm) across.

4 To make the bun wrappers, roll the Dough into a cylinder 1 in (2 cm) in diameter and slice it into 20 equal pieces, each of $1/_2$ in ($1^1/_2$ cm) in length.

5 Place a piece of the Dough on a floured surface and flatten it slightly with your palm. Using a rolling pin, roll it gently with one hand while rotating it in the opposite direction with the other hand, to form a thin circle approximately 4 in (10 cm) in diameter. Roll out all the pieces of Dough in the same manner and set aside on a lightly floured surface or plate.

6 Place a bun wrapper in your palm and top with 1 tablespoon of the Filling. Gather the edges to the middle to enclose the Filling, then pinch the top to seal and twist it slightly. Place each bun, with the pinched side up, on a square piece of baking paper and steam in a steamer for 8 minutes.

Note: *Pau* flour is a highly-bleached, all-purpose flour milled from soft wheat. Steamed buns made with this flour will turn out whiter than when using plain flour. *Pau* flour is available in plastic packets in Asian food stores. If plain flour is used, the buns will appear yellowish when cooked but taste just as good.

Makes 20 buns   Preparation time: 45 minutes   Cooking time: 8 minutes

crisp asparagus rolls with cheese and xo sauce

1. Cut the filo pastry into long rectangular strips. The width of each strip should measure $2/3$ the height of the asparagus spears.

2. Place the cheese and asparagus on a plate. Move the plate to and fro to coat the asparagus with the cheese.

3. Place the asparagus spear on a filo strip and add the XO sauce.

4. Brush the filo strip with melted butter.

5. Roll the filo strip around the spear 3 to 4 times, trim and seal the edge with a dab of butter.

6. Pan-fry the asparagus rolls until golden brown on all sides, placing the sealed edge face down first.

steamed dim sum chicken buns

1. Mix the Dough ingredients and knead into a smooth round dough. Set aside for $1/2$ an hour.

2. Form the Dough into a cylinder (1 in/2 cm in diameter) and slice it into 20 pieces, each of $1/2$ in ($1^{1}/2$ cm) in length.

3. Flatten a piece of dough with the palm of your hand. Roll each piece of dough gently with one hand while rotating it with the other hand, until a thin round bun wrapper is obtained.

4. Place 1 tablespoon of the Filling on each wrapper.

5. Gather the edges of the wrapper to the middle to enclose the Filling and pinch the top to seal and twist it slightly.

honey glazed stuffed chicken wings

1. Push the meat and skin downward to expose the bones.

2. Pull out the bones.

3. Stuff the deboned wing with the Filling.

4. Cut and discard the tip of the chicken wing.

5. Roll the stuffed wing with 3 layers of plastic wrap. While holding the ends of the plastic wrap, continue to roll on the surface until a firm and compact cylinder is obtained.

6. Knot the ends of the plastic wrap near the chicken to seal.

fougasse bread with thai basil and xo sauce

1. Roll each ball of dough to form a 3 x 6-in (7 x 15-cm) rectangle, $\frac{1}{8}$ in (3 mm) thick.

2. Brush the dough with the batter, spread the Sundried Tomato Purée and sprinkle grated gruyére cheese.

3. Fold both ends of the dough, allowing to ovelap at the center. Turn the dough over.

4. With a knife, score 6 diagonal lines through the dough.

5. Stretch the dough by pulling it apart gently with your fingers.

6. Brush the dough with olive oil and top with grated gruyére cheese.

honey glazed stuffed chicken wings

Partially deboned then stuffed with a mixture redolent of five spice powder, white pepper and oyster sauce, these morsels are a pleasing update of that perennial party food staple, the honey glazed chicken wing.

20 chicken wings
1 tablespoon butter
1 to 2 tablespoons honey

Filling
3 oz (100 g) ground chicken meat
3 fresh shiitake mushrooms, stems
   removed and discarded, caps minced
1 spring onion, minced
3 shallots, minced
$1/4$ teaspoon five spice powder
$1/2$ teaspoon ground white pepper
1 teaspoon salt
1 teaspoon oyster sauce
1 teaspoon sesame oil
$1/2$ teaspoon rice wine or sake

Step-by-step photos and instructions for this recipe are provided on page 113.

1 To make the Filling, combine all the ingredients but reserve $1/2$ of the salt and pepper in a bowl and mix well. Set aside.
2 Debone each chicken wing by pushing the skin and meat downward to expose the bones, then pull out the bones, leaving the meat and skin intact.
3 Stuff the deboned wings with the Filling using a small spoon. Cut off and discard the tip of each stuffed wing. On a dry surface, roll each stuffed wing with 3 layers of plastic wrap into a cylinder that is firm and compact. Seal by knotting the ends of the plastic wrap near the chicken.
4 Blanch at high heat for about 10 minutes. Remove and set aside to cool, then unwrap and season the stuffed wings with the remaining salt and pepper.
5 Melt the butter in a skillet and pan-fry the stuffed wings over medium heat until brown on all sides, about 10 minutes. Add the honey and pan-fry for a further minute to coat well. Remove from heat and halve each wing crosswise. Arrange on a platter and serve hot.

Note: The stuffed chicken wings may also be grilled for 15 to 20 minutes. Honey may be added to glaze the chicken during the last 5 minutes of grilling.

Makes 20 pieces   Preparation time: 1 hour   Cooking time: 20 minutes

fougasse bread with thai basil and xo sauce

Fougasse, or "ladder" bread, is an attractive flatbread from the south of France. The sunny flavors of sundried tomatoes permeate the dough here and the addition of gruyére cheese adds yet another interesting dimension to this Mediterranean favorite, while Thai basil and XO sauce add an Asian twist.

$3/_4$ cup (7 oz/200 g) grated gruyére cheese, for sprinkling
Olive oil, for brushing

Dough
$1/_2$ teaspoon instant yeast granules
2 tablespoons warm water
$3/_4$ cup (180 ml) fresh milk
$2/_3$ cup (150 ml) water
$3^1/_2$ cups (500 g) flour
1 tablespoon salt
1 teaspoon olive oil

Sundried Tomato Purée
$3/_4$ cup (7 oz/200 g) sundried tomatoes
4 tablespoons XO sauce
2 tablespoons chopped fresh Thai basil

Batter
5 tablespoons (100 g) softened butter
$1/_3$ cup (125 ml) olive oil
$1^1/_3$ cups (200 g) flour

Step-by-step photos and instructions for this recipe are provided on page 113.

1 First make the Dough by dissolving the instant yeast in 2 tablespoons of warm water. Combine the milk and water, and whisk in the dissolved yeast. Mix in the flour and salt using a mixer at slow speed for 5 minutes. Before the last 30 seconds, add the olive oil. Flour your hands, remove the dough and form it into a ball. Lightly flour the Dough, cover with a cloth and set aside for 30 minutes in a warm place to rise.

2 To make the Sundried Tomato Purée, purée the sundried tomatoes and XO sauce in a blender. Transfer to a bowl, add the Thai basil and mix well. Set aside.

3 To make the Batter, whisk the butter with $1/_3$ cup of the olive oil in a bowl, then fold in the flour. Set aside.

4 Preheat the oven to 400°F (200°C).

5 Flour your hands, divide the Dough into 20 portions and form each into a ball. Using a rolling pin, roll the ball on a lightly floured surface to form a 3 x 6-in (7 x 15-cm) rectangle, $1/_8$ in (3 mm) thick. Brush the top of the rectangular dough with the batter. Spread the Sundried Tomato Purée and sprinkle with $1/_2$ teaspoon of the grated gruyére cheese.

6 Fold both ends of the filled dough, allowing to overlap at the center, then turn it over so that the folded side is at the bottom. Score the back of the filled dough diagonally several times with a knife, cutting through the bottom, then stretch it slightly with your fingers (as shown in the photos on page 113). Place the dough on a baking sheet and brush it with olive oil and sprinkle with gruyére cheese. Repeat the process until all the ingredients are used up.

7 Bake the bread in the oven at 400°F (200°C) for 12 minutes.

Makes 20 pieces   Preparation time: 1 hour   Cooking time: 40 minutes

rice paper sashimi salad rolls

Rice paper sashimi salad rolls are one of Vietnam's culinary gifts to the world. Filled with a lavish assortment of seafood—lobster, sashimi tuna, shrimp and clams, and served with a bracing, wasabi-based dip—these rolls are healthy, light and refined.

6 dried rice paper wrappers (see note)

Filling
1 teaspoon soy sauce
1 teaspoon sesame oil
1 teaspoon salt
1 teaspoon freshly ground black pepper
$1/_2$ tablespoon wasabi paste
$1/_2$ cup (90 g) carrot, cut into thin shreds
$1/_2$ cup (95 g) zucchini, cut into thin shreds
1 tablespoon minced coriander leaves (cilantro)
1 radicchio or romaine lettuce leaf, thinly sliced
1 tablespoon minced chives
5 slices Japanese pickled ginger
$1/_4$ cup sashimi tuna or smoked salmon (about 2 oz/50 g), cut into very thin strips
$1/_4$ cup (40 g) canned or freshly cooked clams
3 boiled shrimp or prawns (20 g), peeled and sliced
3 tablespoons (30 g) cooked lobster meat, thinly sliced

Wasabi Dipping Sauce
2 tablespoons wasabi powder
2 tablespoons water
3 tablespoons soy sauce
2 tablespoons black soy sauce
6 tablespoons *dashi* stock or $1/_2$ teaspoon *dashi* stock granules dissolved in 6 tablespoons hot water.

1 First make the Wasabi Dipping Sauce by dissolving the wasabi powder in the water, then adding all the other ingredients and mixing well. Set aside.

2 To make the Filling, whisk the soy sauce, sesame oil, salt, black pepper and wasabi paste in a large bowl until well blended. Add the sliced vegetables and pickled ginger, and toss to mix well. Set aside for 5 minutes. Add the raw tuna or smoked salmon strips and seafood, and mix until well combined. Set aside.

3 Dip each rice paper wrapper in a bowl of warm water for a few seconds to soften. Remove, dry with paper towels and top with 2 tablespoons of the Filling. Roll one side of the wrapper over the Filling, then fold the ends in and roll up tightly into a cylinder, pressing to seal. Make 6 salad rolls in this manner with all the ingredients.

4 Slice each roll in half and serve chilled with the Wasabi Sauce.

Note: Dried rice paper wrappers are sold in Asian food stores in plastic packets containing 10 or more wrappers. They are round and white, about 10 in (25 cm) in diameter.

Makes 12 pieces   Preparation time: 25 minutes

steamed scallops with black bean dressing

Fresh scallops are a delicate treat and require quick cooking and unfussy embellishments in order to shine. A hint of salty black beans, some sweetish rice wine, a few Asian aromatics and a brief steaming give spectacularly flavorsome results.

12 fresh scallops in their shells
2 spring onions, green part sliced lengthwise into long thin strands and soaked in cold water, to garnish

Black Bean Dressing
2 spring onions, white part minced
2 cloves garlic, minced
2 teaspoons minced fresh young ginger root
1 to 1$^1/_2$ tablespoons black bean garlic sauce (see note)
2 tablespoons rice wine or sake
1$^1/_2$ teaspoons sugar
1 teaspoon olive oil

1 Shuck each scallop and discard the top shell. Rinse under running water to remove sand and dirt. Carefully remove the muscle and organ, leaving only the white flesh. Cut the stem to separate the white flesh from the shell with a paring knife. Stand the white flesh vertically on its shell to drain excess water. Shuck all the scallops in this manner.
2 To make the Black Bean Dressing, combine all the ingredients in a bowl and mix well.
3 Spoon 1 teaspoon of the Black Bean Dressing over each scallop and steam the scallops in their shells in bamboo steaming baskets for 4 minutes, making sure not to crowd or tilt the scallops inside the baskets (for best results, use stacked basket and steam the scallops individually). Serve hot, garnished with spring onions.

Note: The black bean garlic sauce normally used in this dish has large chunks of fermented black soybeans and is sold in small jars in Asian food markets. Whole fermented black beans may also be used with a bit of minced garlic and soy sauce added.

Makes 12 scallops or serves 4   Preparation time: 30 minutes
Cooking time: 4 minutes

spicy fish cakes with coconut and coriander

This is a truely flexible recipe—the fish cake mixture can be either steamed (as shown here) or dropped by the spoonful into hot oil and deep-fried, or pan-fried. The cakes partner well with watercress sauce or, if you prefer, red bell pepper sauce.

10 oz (300 g) white fish fillets (snapper, seabass, halibut, sole)
4 tablespoons coconut cream
1 egg
2 tablespoons chopped coriander leaves (cilantro)
2 cloves garlic, crushed
2 bird's-eye chilies
1 spring onion, minced
Lettuce leaves, for steaming
Crispy Fried Leek (see note), to garnish

Watercress Sauce
1 bunch (100 g) watercress, stems removed
2 cups (500 ml) water
1 teaspoon salt
Ice water
4 tablespoons chicken stock or $1/4$ teaspoon chicken stock powder dissolved in 4 tablespoons hot water
1 tablespoon *yuzu* juice or a mixture of Mandarin orange and lemon juice

1 To make the Watercress Sauce, blanch the watercress in water and salt for about 3 minutes. Remove from heat and plunge in ice water to stop further cooking. Strain and squeeze the blanched watercress to remove the liquid. Purée the watercress with 2 tablespoons of the chicken stock and *yuzu* into a smooth paste with a blender. Transfer to a bowl and whisk in the remaining chicken stock until well combined.
2 Grind $2/3$ of the fish fillets, coconut cream, egg, coriander leaves, garlic, chilies and spring onion until semi-smooth in a blender. Set aside.
3 Slice the other $1/3$ of the fish fillets very finely.
4 Combine the ground mixture and chopped fish in a bowl and mix well. Wet your hands and form the mixture into small patties.
5 Steam in a steamer lined with lettuce or vegetable leaves for 10 minutes until cooked. Serve the fish cakes with Watercress Sauce or Red Bell Pepper Sauce (see page 100), garnished with the Crispy Fried Leek.
6 Alternatively, you may deep-fry or pan-fry the patties over low heat in 1 tablespoon of olive oil in a skillet, about 3 minutes on each side.

Note: To make the Crispy Fried Leek, thinly slice 1 leek and deep-fry in a pan over medium heat for about 2 to 3 minutes, stirring constantly, until golden brown and crispy. Remove and drain on paper towels.

Makes 12 cakes   Preparation time: 20 minutes   Cooking time: 10 to 15 minutes

pork satays with pineapple and spicy peanut sauce

Satay comes loaded with flavor and this recipe is no exception. From the spicy marinade to the fullness of peanut sauce and the lusciousness of pineapple, these are destined to become everyone's favorite.

14 oz (400 g) pork fillets or loin, sliced
  into 1 x 5 in (3 x 12 cm) strips
2 cups fresh or canned pineapple cubes
24 bamboo skewers (see note)
1 tablespoon oil, for grilling

Marinade
1 tablespoon soy sauce
1 tablespoon rice wine or sake
4 cloves garlic, minced
1 teaspoon sesame oil
1 teaspoon five spice powder
$1/2$ teaspoon freshly ground black pepper
1 tablespoon sugar
$1/2$ teaspoon salt

Spicy Peanut Sauce
4 small shallots
4 cloves garlic
2 tablespoons soy sauce
2 tablespoons olive oil
2 in (5 cm) fresh ginger root, sliced
2 red chili peppers, sliced
2 tablespoons black soy sauce
2 teaspoons sugar
2 cups (500 ml) water
2 cups roasted unsalted peanuts

1 To make the Spicy Peanut Sauce, grind all the ingredients in a blender or food processor to a coarse paste. Bring the mixture to a rolling boil in a saucepan over high heat. Reduce heat to low and simmer for about 45 minutes, stirring occasionally, until the mixture has reduced to half. Remove and set aside.

2 Mix all the Marinade ingredients together in a bowl and stir well until the sugar is dissolved. Marinate the pork strips in the Marinade for at least 5 hours or overnight in the refrigerator.

3 Thread each pork strip, followed by a pineapple cube, onto a bamboo skewer. Thread all the ingredients onto skewers in this manner. Grill the skewers, a few at a time, on a charcoal or pan grill over medium heat, basting with a little oil for about 3 minutes on each side until cooked.

4 Serve hot with Spicy Peanut Sauce.

Note: If grilling the satays over charcoal, soak the bamboo skewers in water for 1 hour before using to keep them from burning.

Makes 24 skewers   Preparation time: 15 minutes + overnight marination
Cooking Time: 1 hour

spicy crab salad sandwiches

Cucumber sandwiches are an old idea but a fabulous one, especially when reinvented and given a modern, Asian twist. Use good quality, fresh bread rolls and assemble these just before you wish to serve them or the bread will become soggy.

9 oz (250 g) Japanese or baby cucumbers
1/4 teaspoon salt
5 oz (150 g) fresh cooked or canned crabmeat (1 cup)
2 tablespoons lemon or lime juice
1/2 teaspoon ground white pepper
4 fresh tofu buns or poppy seed bread or all grain bread rolls
1 teaspoon finely sliced Thai basil leaves, to serve

Chili Dressing
1 to 2 tablespoons minced red chili
2 cloves garlic, minced
6 shallots or 1 small onion, minced
1/2 cup (125 ml) water
1 1/2 tablespoons sugar
2 teaspoons fish sauce

1 To make the Chili Dressing, combine all the ingredients in a saucepan and simmer over high heat for about 6 minutes, stirring occasionally, until the mixture has thickened. Remove and set aside to cool.

2 Peel the cucumbers, then slice very thinly. If using larger cucumbers, cut in half lengthwise first, scrape out the seeds with a spoon before slicing the cucumbers. Rub the salt into the cucumber slices and mix well, then strain or squeeze the cucumber to remove the liquid. Add all but 1 tablespoon of the Chili Dressing, crabmeat, lemon or lime juice and pepper to the cucumber slices and toss to combine.

3 Make a slit in the bread rolls and stuff each roll with the cucumber crab salad mixture, top with the reserved Chili Dressing and basil leaves.

Note: Japanese cucumbers are very small and crunchy, and almost seedless. Baby cucumbers or fresh pickling gherkins make a good substitute.

Makes 4 pieces   Preparation time: 20 minutes   Cooking time: 6 minutes

spicy tuna tataki rolls

Purchase sashimi-grade tuna and you will be assured of the freshness and quality of fish that this recipe, a cunning synthesis of Japanese and Vietnamese influences, deserves.

1 lb (500 g) fresh sashimi tuna fillets
$1/2$ tablespoon olive oil
3 tablespoons soy sauce combined with
  1 teaspoon wasabi powder or $1/2$ teaspoon wasabi paste, for dipping

Spice Paste
2 bird's-eye chilies
4 cloves garlic
12 coriander leaves (cilantro)
3 spring onions
$1^1/2$ tablespoons *yuzu* or mixture of
  mandarin orange and lemon juice
$1/2$ tablespoon olive oil

1 To make the Spice Paste, grind the chilies, garlic, coriander leaves (cilantro) and spring onions to a smooth paste in a blender. Transfer to a bowl, stir in the *yuzu* and olive oil. Set aside.

2 Slice the tuna into 10 thin rectangular strips, each measuring around 1 x 3 in ($2^1/2$ x 7 cm) and approximately $1/8$ in (3 mm) thick.

3 Spread $1/2$ teaspoon of the Spice Paste on one side of each tuna strip and roll it into a cylinder. Roll all the tuna strips in this manner.

4. Place the tuna rolls on a fireproof pan and using a torch, sear each tuna roll for about 30 seconds.

5 Arrange the tuna rolls on a platter and serve with dipping bowls of the soy sauce and wasabi mixture.

Note: If you do not have a torch, you may briefly glaze the tuna rolls in a very hot broiler instead.

Makes 10 rolls   Preparation time: 20 minutes   Cooking time: 5 minutes

malaysian beef satays with spicy peanut sauce

Complex spicing is reflective of Malay cuisine, hinting at the many influences that have shaped it over the centuries. The ingredient list here may appear daunting but once everything is measured out and assembled, the actual cooking time is short and the results, sensational.

4 small shallots, minced
4 cloves garlic, minced
4 tablespoons soy sauce
2 tablespoons olive oil
2 teaspoons freshly ground black pepper
4 teaspoons ground cumin
4 teaspoons ground turmeric
4 teaspoons ground fennel
4 teaspoons grated lemon rind
4 teaspoons ground coriander
$1^1/_2$ lbs (700 g) beef tenderloin, cut into cubes
12 bamboo skewers (see note)

Spicy Peanut Sauce
4 small shallots
4 cloves garlic
2 tablespoons soy sauce
2 tablespoons olive oil
2 in (5 cm) fresh ginger root, sliced
2 red chili peppers
2 tablespoons black soy sauce
2 teaspoons sugar
2 cups (500 ml) water
2 cups roasted unsalted peanuts

1 To make the Spicy Peanut Sauce, grind all the ingredients in a blender or food processor to a coarse paste. Bring the mixture to a rolling boil in a saucepan over high heat. Reduce heat to low and simmer for about 45 minutes, stirring occasionally, until the mixture has reduced to half. Remove and set aside.
2 Combine the shallots, garlic, soy sauce, olive oil, black pepper, cumin, turmeric, fennel, lemon rind and coriander in a bowl and mix well. Coat the beef cubes with the mixture and thread onto the bamboo skewers.
3 Grill the satays, a few at a time, on a charcoal or pan grill over medium heat for about 3 minutes on each side until cooked. Serve hot with Spicy Peanut Sauce.

Note: If grilling the satays over charcoal, soak the bamboo skewers in water for 1 hour before using to keep them from burning.

Makes 12 sticks   Preparation time: 30 minutes   Cooking time: 1 hour

focaccia buns with thai basil and olives

Focaccia is a flatbread, originally from the Liguria region of north western Italy, which has now become popular all over the world. This version adds the wonderful fragrance of Thai basil.

Pre-ferment Dough
$1/_8$ teaspoon instant yeast granules
1 cup (250 ml) warm water
$1^1/_4$ cups (175 g) flour

Dough
$1/_2$ tablespoon instant yeast granules
2 cups (300 g) flour
$1/_2$ cup (125 ml) ice water
$1/_2$ tablespoon salt
2 tablespoons olive oil
1 cup (100 g) pitted black olives
1 tablespoon minced fresh Thai basil or
    sweet basil

1 To make the Pre-ferment Dough, whisk the yeast with warm water in a bowl until it dissolves. Fold in the flour until well combined. Cover the bowl with a cloth and set aside for 1 hour, leaving the Pre-ferment Dough to double in size.
2 Preheat the oven to 400°F (200°C).
3 To make the Dough, dissolve the instant yeast in 2 tablespoons of warm water. Mix the dissolved yeast, flour and rested Pre-ferment Dough in a mixer at slow speed for about 1 minute, adding in the ice water gradually, followed by the salt and beating well between each addition. Add the olive oil, increase speed to medium and continue mixing for another 15 minutes. Add the black olives and basil leaves, and mix for a further 2 minutes. Flour your hand, remove the dough and pack into a lightly floured rectangular pan. Cover with a cloth and let it rest for 30 minutes.
4 Transfer the Dough onto a floured surface and lightly flour the top. Halve the Dough lengthwise and cut each half into 4 x 2 in (20 x 5 cm) rectangles or 4-in (10-cm) triangles. Bake in the oven at 400°F (200°C) for 15 minutes.

Makes 20 buns   Preparation time: 30 minutes + $1^1/_2$ hours fermenting
Cooking time: 15 minutes

vegetarian rice paper rolls

Mediterranean touches—sundried tomatoes, black olives and olive oil—blend surprisingly well with mild tofu, black Chinese mushrooms, Chinese fungus and rice vermicelli. Any mushroom actually works well here (chanterelles or morels, for example). The striking presentation makes these rolls ideal to serve as a shared appetizer or as an accompaniment to pre-dinner drinks.

3 tablespoons cornstarch
1 egg, beaten
15 dried rice paper wrappers (see note)
Oil for deep-frying

Vegetarian Filling
3 oz (100 g) dried rice vermicelli
2 cups (500 ml) water
2 teaspoons olive oil
2 teaspoons salt
9 oz (250 g) firm tofu, pan-fried and shredded
6 dried black Chinese mushrooms, soaked in warm water to soften, stems discarded, caps diced
10 pieces dried black fungus (about 15 g), soaked in water to soften, thinly sliced
1 small carrot, sliced into thin strips
$1/2$ cup (40 g) sundried tomatoes, thinly sliced
10 pitted black olives, diced
$1/2$ teaspoon ground white pepper
2 tablespoons minced coriander leaves (cilantro)

Chili Garlic Dipping Sauce
3 tablespoons minced red chili
2 tablespoons minced garlic
1 teaspoon sugar
2 tablespoons black vinegar
$1/4$ cup (60 ml) fish sauce

1 Make the Chili Garlic Dipping Sauce by combining all the ingredients in a bowl and mixing well. Transfer to a serving bowl and set aside. This makes about $1/2$ cup of sauce.
2 To make the Vegetarian Filling, break the dried rice vermicelli into pieces and boil in the water, olive oil and 1 teaspoon salt in a large pot for about 2 minutes, then drain well in a colander. Mix the rice vermicelli with all the other ingredients in a large bowl until well combined.
3 Combine the cornstarch and beaten egg in a bowl and mix well. Set aside.
4 Dip 1 rice paper wrapper in a large bowl of warm water for a few seconds to soften. Scoop 3 tablespoons of the Vegetarian Filling onto the wrapper and fold one side over the Vegetarian Filling, then fold in both ends, and roll up tightly into a cylinder. Seal the edge with a dab of the egg and constarch mixture. Repeat until all the ingredients are used up.
5 Deep-fry the rolls over medium heat until golden brown on all sides, about 5 minutes each. Cut each roll into half and arrange on a platter. Serve hot with the Chili Garlic Dipping Sauce.

Note: Dried rice paper wrappers are sold in Asian food stores in plastic packets containing 10 or more wrappers. They are round and white, about 10 in (25 cm) in diameter.

Makes 30 pieces   Preparation time: 1 hour   Cooking time: 20 minutes

foie gras fried rice

Foie Gras is one of the world's great luxury foods and should be treated with minimal fuss in order to be fully enjoyed. Tossing it through this tasty fried rice will highlight its impossibly smooth, super-rich characteristics.

5 oz (150 g) duck foie gras
$1/2$ cup (70 g) flour
Oil for deep-frying
2 shallots, minced
1 egg, beaten
2 cups (400 g) cooked Thai fragrant rice
$3/4$ cup (90 g) diced fresh asparagus
$1/2$ cup (90 g) diced carrot
$1/2$ cup (50 g) fresh uncooked corn kernels cut from a cob of corn
1 teaspoon salt
$1/2$ teaspoon ground white pepper
$1/2$ teaspoon sesame oil
2 spring onions, thinly sliced, to garnish

1 Remove the outer membrane, if any, from the foie gras and dice it using a knife dipped in hot water. Coat the foie gras dice with the flour and deep-fry over very high heat for 30 seconds. Remove with a wire basket and drain on paper towels. Set aside.
2 Place 2 tablespoons of the oil in a wok and stir-fry the shallots over high heat until golden brown and translucent, about 30 seconds. Add the egg and scramble until semi-firm, then add the rice and stir-fry for about 1 minute to mix well. Add the vegetables and stir-fry for several minutes, seasoning with the salt, pepper and sesame oil. Add the foie gras and toss well. Serve warm, garnished with sliced spring onions.

Makes 10 small tasting portions   Preparation time: 20 minutes
Cooking time: 15 minutes

savory lemongrass mousse

The unmistakable citrusy tang of lemongrass perfumes this delicious mousse; serve it as a dinner party first course. Agar-agar ensures a creamy, soft consistency while toasted bread and spiced sausage provide a surprise element of crunch.

5 stalks lemongrass, thick bottom third only, outer layers discarded, inner part quartered and bruised
2 cups (500 ml) chicken stock or 1 chicken stock cube dissolved in 2 cups (500 ml) hot water
5 star anise
1/4 teaspoon salt
1 tablespoon agar-agar powder
Large bowl of ice cubes
1 cup (250 ml) whipping cream
2 cups (500 ml) cream
2 tablespoons lime juice
1 tablespoon minced chives
1 medium tomato, blanched then peeled and deseeded, flesh diced
1/4 teaspoon freshly ground black pepper
Toasted bread sticks, to serve
Thinly sliced and baked chorizo sausage, to serve

1 Boil the lemongrass, chicken stock, star anise and salt in a saucepan over high heat until the sauce has reduced to half, about 6 minutes. Remove and strain into a small saucepan. Simmer the mixture over low heat and whisk in the agar-agar powder until it is fully dissolved. Remove from the heat and place the saucepan on top of a large bowl of ice cubes to cool, stirring continuously until the mixture thickens. Set aside.
2 Whip the 2 types of cream with a mixer until stiff. Whisk 1/2 of the cream into the agar-agar mixture until well blended and add the lime juice to the remaining whipped cream. Finally, fold both mixtures together.
3 Spoon the mousse into small serving cups and top with the minced chives, diced tomato and a sprinkling of black pepper. Serve with toasted bread sticks and baked slices of chorizo sausage.

Makes 24 portions   Preparation time: 20 minutes   Cooking time: 8 minutes

shiitake stuffed squid rings

Purchase whole, fresh squids for this pretty dish; ask your fishmonger to clean the squids for you, if you prefer, making sure he leaves the fins attached. Briefly freezing the squids will actually improve their texture, after which they will bake to tender perfection and yield neat, compact slices as shown.

1 lb (500 g) fresh whole medium squids, measuring from 1 1/2 in (4 cm) to 2 in (5 cm) in diameter (see note)

4 teaspoons olive oil

8 to 10 fresh shiitake mushrooms (4 oz/ 125 g), stems removed and discarded, caps diced

2 to 3 tablespoons diced sundried tomatoes

1 clove garlic, crushed

1 medium onion, diced

1 tablespoon butter

2 slices dried or lightly toasted bread, crusts trimmed, cut into 1/2 in (1 cm) cubes for croutons

2 large fresh tomatoes (about 9 oz/ 250 g), blanched, peeled and deseeded, flesh diced

2 tablespoons minced parsley

2 tablespoons minced coriander leaves (cilantro)

5 pitted black olives, minced

1 spring onion, thinly sliced

1 tablespoon minced fresh ginger root

1/4 teaspoon salt

1/2 teaspoon pepper

16 toothpicks or skewers

1 Preheat the oven to 400°F (200°C).

2 Remove the head and reddish-brown skin from the squids and pull off the fins. Slice the fins into small cubes and stir-fry in a skillet over high heat in 1 teaspoon of the olive oil for 10 seconds. Remove and set aside to cool.

3 Heat 1 teaspoon of the olive oil in a skillet and stir-fry the mushrooms, sundried tomatoes, garlic and 1/2 of the onion over very high heat for 20 seconds. Remove and set aside to cool.

4 To make the croutons, heat 1 teaspoon of the olive oil and 1/2 of the butter in a skillet over medium heat and fry the bread cubes until light brown, turning frequently to ensure even browning on all sides. Remove and drain on paper towels.

5 Combine the stir-fried squid cubes, mushroom mixture, croutons and other ingredients in a mixing bowl and mix thoroughly. Stuff the body sacs of the squids, packing the filling in tightly but leaving about 1 in (2 cm) at the open ends. Seal the open ends with toothpicks or skewers.

6 Heat the remaining olive oil in a skillet over low heat and pan-fry the stuffed squids for about 5 minutes, turning to brown both sides. Remove and brush with the remaining butter. Wrap the squids in aluminum foil and bake in the oven for 15 minutes at 400°F (200°C). Slice the squids into 1/2-in (1-cm) segments and serve.

Note: To improve the texture of the squids, making them less chewy, freeze the fresh squids for a day prior to use.

Makes 16 pieces   Preparation time: 60 minutes   Cooking time: 25 minutes

chicken and coriander corn fritters

Many cultures share a love of corn cakes or fritters in one guise or another. These golden nuggets explode with the flavors of fresh corn kernels, chicken, coriander and fish sauce.

2 ears (1 lb/500 g) fresh corn or 2 cups canned or frozen whole corn kernels
4 tablespoons minced coriander leaves (cilantro)
1 tablespoon cornstarch
2 eggs
4 cloves garlic, minced
2 teaspoons freshly ground black pepper
$1/4$ teaspoon salt
1 teaspoon sugar
1 to 2 tablespoons fish sauce
9 oz (250 g) ground chicken
Oil for deep-frying
Chicory, to garnish
Sweet Thai chili sauce (see page 35), to serve

1 If using fresh corn, husk it and cut the kernels from the cobs with a knife.
2 Combine $1/2$ of the fresh corn or canned corn kernels, coriander leaves, constarch, eggs, garlic, black pepper, salt, sugar and fish sauce in a deep bowl. Mix well and process in a blender or food processor until smooth. Add the mixture to the remaining fresh or canned corn kernels and the ground chicken. Mix with the hands until well combined. Set aside.
3 Heat the oil until hot. Gently drop 1 tablespoon of the corn mixture into the oil at a time and deep-fry for 3 minutes each or until golden brown. Remove and drain on paper towels. Garnish with chicory and serve warm with sweet Thai chili sauce.

Makes 24 pieces   Preparation time: 25 minutes   Cooking time: 10 minutes

caramelized green mango and octopus skewers

Brief poaching in a light chili-ginger syrup accentuates the fruity tartness of green mangoes. These are generally used shredded, in salads, so their presentation here in larger pieces, threaded on skewers with neat pieces of octopus, is an original, and stylish, departure.

6 cups (1¹/₂ liters) water
Juice of 1 lemon
10 sprigs fresh thyme
10 oz (300 g) fresh octopus (tentacles only)
Ice water
12 small bamboo or stainless skewers
Mizuna or salad greens, to garnish
White sesame seeds, to garnish
Chicken Rice Chili Sauce (see page 155), for dipping
¹/₂ tablespoon olive oil

Caramelized Green Mango
1 cup (250 ml) water
1 teaspoon fish sauce
¹/₃ cup (65 g) sugar
2 red chilies, minced
1 teaspoon minced fresh ginger root
2 unripe mangoes (14 oz/400 g in total), peeled and cut into chunks

1 Bring the water to a boil in a pot and add the lemon juice and thyme sprigs. Place the octopus in the boiling water and simmer for 1 hour. Drain the octopus and plunge into ice water to cool. Slice the octopus into bite-sized cubes and set aside.

2 To make the Caramelized Green Mango, combine the water, fish sauce, sugar, chili and ginger in a saucepan and bring to a boil. Reduce heat to low and add the mango chunks. Simmer for about 3 minutes, stirring constantly, until the sauce caramelizes and coats the mango chunks.

3 Thread each skewer with alternating chunks of the octopus and the mango. Serve garnished with mizuna leaves or salad greens and white sesame seeds, accompanied by dipping bowls of Chicken Rice Chili Sauce mixed with olive oil.

Note: To save time, cooked octopus may be used and is available in Japanese seafood shops. Raw baby squid may also be substituted for the octopus. To prepare the baby squid, detach and discard the head, remove the cartilage in the center of the tentacles. Remove the reddish-brown skin from the body sac and scrape the inside of the body sac with a dull edge of a knife. Rinse well and slice the body sac and tentacles into bite-sized pieces.

Makes 12 skewers   Preparation time: 35 minutes   Cooking time: 1 hour 15 minutes

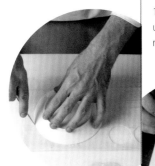

1. Roll out the filo pastry on a dry surface and use a small knife to cut around the saucer and ramekin.

2. Brush a large pastry circle with the melted butter.

3. Place a large pastry circle in a ramekin mould.

4. Place 2 tablespoons of the Filling into the mould and press lightly with a spoon.

7. Seal the folded side with a small pastry circle, pressing gently.

5. Fold the edges of the pastry inward to enclose the Filling.

8. Remove the pie from the mould.

6. Brush the folded side with a bit of melted butter.

9. Place another large buttered pastry circle into the mould, place the pie inside and fold the edges to enclose.

10. Brush the top with melted butter and seal with a small pastry circle.

vegetable and seafood pastillas

Elegant, individual pies with a fine, crisp filo crust are just the thing for an al fresco lunch or dinner party starter. Prime seafood and summer vegetables are embellished by the merest hint of black bean garlic sauce, allowing their natural flavors to sing.

10 sheets filo pastry (20 x 11 in/50 x 28 cm each)
2 to 3 tablespoons (60 g) unsalted butter
Salad greens, to garnish

Filling
$1^1/_4$ cups cubed eggplant (about 150 g)
4 fresh shiitake mushrooms, caps diced
$1^1/_4$ cups diced zucchini (about 150 g)
$^1/_2$ red bell pepper, diced
1 teaspoon salt and pepper
3 tablespoons olive oil
2 shallots, minced
2 to 3 cloves garlic, minced
3 fresh scallops, diced
3 oz (100 g) fresh shrimp, peeled and diced
1 tablespoon black bean and garlic sauce

Step-by-step photos and instructions for this recipe are provided on the opposite page.

1 To make the Filling, season the cut vegetables with some salt and pepper. Heat 1 tablespoon of the olive oil in a skillet over medium heat and stir-fry the eggplant and mushrooms until soft, about 3 minutes. Remove and set aside. Repeat with the zucchini and bell pepper, then combine all the stir-fried vegetables in a bowl and mix well. Set aside.
2 Heat the remaining olive oil in a skillet over medium heat and sauté the shallots and garlic for about 1 minute until golden brown and fragrant. Add the seafood and stir-fry for about 1 minute until the shrimp turns pink. Remove and add to the vegetable mixture. Stir in the black bean garlic chili sauce and toss until well blended. Set aside.
3 Melt the butter in a saucepan. Set aside.
4 Roll out the filo pastry on a dry surface and using a small knife, cut out 20 large circles, about 6 in (15 cm) in diameter and 20 small circles, about $2^1/_2$ in (6 cm) in diameter using a saucer and a small ramekin to outline.
5 To make each pie, brush a large pastry circle with the melted butter and place it in a ramekin mould, then top with 2 tablespoons of the Filling. Fold the edges of the pastry inward and brush with a bit of melted butter, then seal the folded side with a small pastry circle. Remove the pie from the mould and repeat the process to wrap it with another layer of big and small pastry circles. Repeat until all the ingredients are used up.
6 Pan-fry the pies with the remaining butter in a skillet over low heat until golden brown, about 5 minutes on each side. Serve on a platter, garnished with fresh salad greens.

Note: Bottled black bean and garlic sauce is sold in well stocked supermarket. If not available, you may soak 1 tablespoon salted black beans in water for 20 minutes, mince and add to the recipe.

Makes 10 pieces   Preparation time: 30 minutes   Cooking time: 25 minutes

asparagus spears with chicken in clear tofu broth

A light body and full flavor are the hallmarks of many Asian soups; it is important to start with a stock that is clear and extremely tasty. Tofu and clever use of chicken and asparagus add substance and drama to this stunning soup.

5 oz (150 g) ground chicken
2 tablespoons minced watercress
2 tablespoons minced coriander leaves (cilantro)
5 cloves garlic, minced
1 teaspoon potato flour or $^1/_2$ teaspoon cornstarch
$^1/_2$ tablespoon soy sauce
$^1/_2$ tablespoon ground white pepper
$^1/_4$ teaspoon salt
8 young asparagus spears (4 oz/125 g), bottom one-third cut off and discarded
2 cups (500 ml) chicken stock or 1 chicken stock cube dissolved in 2 cups (500 ml) hot water
2 tablespoons diced carrot
$^1/_2$ cup (60 g) firm tofu cubes
1 teaspoon fish sauce

1 Combine the chicken, watercress and coriander leaves in a bowl. Add the garlic, potato flour or cornstarch, soy sauce, pepper and salt, and mix well.
2 Wet your hands, scoop 1 tablespoon of the chicken mixture and wrap it around the base of an asparagus spear. Repeat until the chicken mixture is used up.
3 Bring the chicken stock to a boil in a pot. Add the carrot and tofu. Reduce heat to low and carefully lower the asparagus spears into the chicken broth, ensuring that the spears do not touch one another. Simmer for 3 minutes, turning occasionally. Remove the asparagus spears from the broth and gently stir in the fish sauce.
4 Serve hot in 8 individual serving bowls, each with some soup, tofu, carrot and 1 asparagus spear.

Makes 8 portions   Preparation time: 20 minutes   Cooking time: 5 minutes

honey glazed pumpkin wedges

The soft sweetness of pumpkin marries wonderfully with the distinctive notes of soy sauce, ginger and sesame. Easy to prepare and perfectly transportable, this is an ideal dish to take on a casual picnic. Alternatively, serve as a side dish for lamb or chicken.

1 small pumpkin (about 1$^1/_2$ lbs/700 g)
1 tablespoon (20 g) butter
1 teaspoon fresh ginger, cut into thin shreds
2 tablespoons sake
$^1/_4$ teaspoon salt
$^1/_3$ cup (80 ml) water
3 tablespoons honey
2 tablespoons soy sauce
2 teaspoons sesame seeds (if possible, a mixture of black and white seeds)
Lime and orange zest, to garnish

1 Peel and halve the pumpkin, then scoop out the seeds with a spoon. Cut the pumpkin into segments, then into small wedges.
2 Melt the butter in a wok or pan over high heat, then add the pumpkin wedges, $^1/_2$ of the ginger, 1 tablespoon sake, salt and water, and mix well. Cover and simmer for 3 minutes, then reduce heat to medium and continue to simmer until the sauce has evaporated. Remove and transfer the pumpkin to a wide plate and set aside to cool.
3 Whisk the honey, soy sauce, remaining ginger and sake in a pan over medium heat for about 2 minutes until well combined. Remove and pour over the cooked pumpkin, then toss well, ensuring that all pieces of the pumpkin are coated. Finally, sprinkle the sesame seeds on top and garnish with lime and orange zest.

Serves 8   Preparation time: 20 minutes   Cooking time: 10 minutes

roast duck vegetable rolls with lemon soy dipping sauce

Crunchy vegetables, sticky-sweet *hoisin* sauce and juicy slices of roast duck create a pleasing interplay of tastes and textures. Use roast duck purchased from a Chinese barbecue shop.

1 cup (60 g) bean sprouts, heads and
   tails removed
2 fresh shiitake mushrooms, stems
   removed and discarded, caps sliced
10 baby asparagus spears, cut into
   lengths
2 cloves garlic, minced
$1/2$ tablespoon sesame oil
1 teaspoon salt
1 teaspoon ground white pepper
5 large Chinese cabbage leaves
4 cups (1 liter) water
Ice water
Roast duck breast (4 oz/125 g)
3 tablespoons *hoisin* sauce
1 red chili, deseeded and sliced into
   strips, to garnish
Sprigs of chervil, to garnish

Lemon Soy Dipping Sauce
6 tablespoons lemon juice
2 tablespoons chili garlic sauce
1 tablespoon black soy sauce
1 tablespoon soy sauce
1 tablespoon sugar

1 To make the Lemon Soy Dipping Sauce, combine all the ingredients in a bowl and mix well. Transfer to a serving bowl and set aside.
2 Mix the bean sprouts, mushrooms, asparagus, garlic, sesame oil, $1/2$ teaspoon of the salt and the pepper in a bowl until well combined, and stir-fry in a wok over high heat for 1 to 2 minutes until just done. Remove from heat and set aside.
3 Cut the thick bottom parts of the Chinese cabbage leaves and reserve the leafy top parts. Slice the stems into thin shreds, add to the stir-fried vegetables, and toss to mix well.
4 Blanch the 5 leafy top parts of the cabbage leaves in a pot with the water and remaining salt for 30 seconds to barely soften, and immediately plunge into ice water to stop cooking. Spread out the blanched leaves and pat dry with paper towels. Set aside.
5 Slice the roast duck breast into long thin strips. Season the duck slices with $1/2$ tablespoon of the *hoisin* sauce and remaining pepper. Set aside.
6 Slice each blanched cabbage leaf in half vertically and remove the stiff central stems to obtain 10 rectangular sheets. Place $1/2$ tablespoon of the vegetable mixture on each sheet, followed by 3 to 4 duck strips and another $1/2$ tablespoon of the vegetable mixture, then roll up tightly into a cylinder and trim both ends so that the roll can stand on its end. Repeat the process with all the ingredients to obtain 10 duck rolls.
7 Garnish the duck rolls with chili strips and chervil, and serve with the Lemon Soy Dipping Sauce or remaining *hoisin* sauce.

Makes 10 rolls   Preparation time: 40 minutes   Cooking time: 5 minutes

steamed chicken meatballs in a fluffy rice coating

Chicken rice is arguably the national dish of Singapore and chicken meatballs with rice are a snack version popularized by the *nyonya* Chinese in Malacca. Originally made the size of tennis balls, proportions have become decidedly dainty over the years, as in this version where water chestnuts add a welcome crunch.

10 oz (300 g) ground chicken
1 tablespoon minced coriander leaves
  (cilantro)
2 teaspoons minced spring onion
4 water chestnuts, peeled and minced
$1/4$ teaspoon salt
$1/4$ teaspoon ground white pepper
1 teaspoon sesame oil
$1/2$ tablespoon rice wine or sake
1 tablespoon cornstarch
1 egg white
1 cup (200 g) uncooked rice, soaked in
  2 cups (500 ml) hot water for 15 to 20
  minutes, drained and set aside
4 pandanus leaves, for steaming (optional)
Soy sauce, for dipping
1 tablespoon sesame seeds

Chicken Rice Chili Sauce
8 red chilies, deseeded and sliced
3 cloves garlic, halved
1 red shallot, chopped
$1^1/2$ in (4 cm) fresh ginger root, sliced
1 tablespoon white vinegar
1 tablespoon lime juice
$1/2$ teaspoon grated lime zest
$1/2$ tablespoon white sesame seeds,
  lightly roasted
1 tablespoon minced coriander leaves
  (cilantro)
$1^1/2$ tablespoons sesame oil
$1/2$ teaspoon salt

1 First make the Chicken Rice Chili Sauce by grinding the chilies, garlic, shallot and ginger to a coarse paste in a blender (do not purée). Transfer to a bowl, stir in the remaining ingredients and mix well. This makes about $1/2$ cup of sauce.

2 Combine the chicken with the coriander leaves, spring onion, water chestnuts, salt, pepper, sesame oil, rice wine or sake, cornstarch and egg white, and mix well.

3 Place the soaked rice on a plate. Wet your hands, scoop 1 tablespoon of the meat mixture and form it very roughly into a meatball. Roll the ball in the soaked rice to lightly coat with grains of rice on all sides. Continue until the meat mixture is used up.

4 Line a steamer tray with pandanus leaves (if using) and steam the rice-coated meatballs over rapidly boiling water for 8 minutes.

5 Serve with separate dipping bowls of Chicken Rice Chili Sauce and soy sauce sprinkled with sesame seeds.

Note: Cover the meatballs with a damp cloth or plastic wrap if you are not serving them immediately, as the rice will otherwise dry out very quickly.

Makes 24 balls   Preparation time: 20 minutes   Cooking time: 8 minutes

sweet coconut tarts

The ambrosial flavor of coconut is the very essence of tropical cuisines—as the juice, milk and flesh of the coconut are all utilized. The unmistakable, sweet savor of desiccated coconut is baked into these dainty little tarts, making them the perfect thing to serve with a relaxing cup of tea or coffee.

2 sheets (1$^1/_2$ lbs/1$^1/_4$ kg) puff pastry
4 teaspoons honey (optional)

Coconut Filling
1$^1/_3$ cups (250 g) sugar
$^3/_4$ cup (200 ml) water
2 cups (150 g) sweetened desiccated
  coconut
2 eggs
$^1/_2$ cup (50 g) custard powder
2 tablespoons (40 g) butter
$^1/_4$ teaspoon baking powder

1 To make the Coconut Filling, heat the sugar and water in a saucepan over medium heat, stirring continuously until the sugar dissolves. Remove and set aside to cool. When the sugar syrup has cooled, add all the other ingredients, stir well and set aside.
2 Preheat the oven to 350°F (180°C).
3 Roll the puff pastry on a well floured surface into thin sheets, about $^1/_8$ in (3 mm) thick. Cut into 2-in (5-cm) circles with a round, fluted cutter. Gently press each pastry circle into the well of a miniature tart mould.
4 Fill each tart mould with 1$^1/_2$ teaspoons of the Coconut Filling. Bake the tarts in the preheated oven at 350°F (180°C) for 20 minutes, until the Coconut Filling rises, browns and cracks at the top. Remove from the oven and set aside to cool. Remove the tarts from the tart moulds and set aside to cool for a further 2 minutes before brushing the tops with honey (if using).

Makes 50 miniature tarts   Preparation time: 20 minutes   Cooking time: 20 minutes

steamed tomato and olive dumplings

Creative use of western ingredients—fresh and sundried tomatoes and olives—meets the simplicity of oriental steaming techniques, and the results are these beautiful and easily made dumplings. Using purchased wonton wrappers is the secret of the super-quick preparation here, while lining your steam basket with cabbage leaves will keep the dumplings from sticking to it.

1 egg yolk
1 tablespoon cornstarch
8 square wonton wrappers
2 to 3 large cabbage leaves, for steaming
1 tablespoon sweet black soy sauce
1 tablespoon balsamic vinegar
Romaine lettuce, to garnish

Filling
2 fresh medium tomatoes (about 4 oz/125 g), blanched, peeled and deseeded, flesh diced
4 shallots, minced
3 to 4 tablespoons sliced sundried tomatoes
12 pitted black olives, diced
3 tablespoons (20 g) minced spring onions
$1/4$ teaspoon salt
$1/4$ teaspoon ground white pepper

1 To make the Filling, combine the tomatoes, shallots, sundried tomatoes, black olives and spring onions in a bowl and mix well, then season with the salt and pepper. Set aside.
2 Mix the egg yolk and cornstarch together. Place 1 tablespoon of the Filling on a wonton wrapper. Fold the wrapper diagonally over the Filling and using your fingers, seal the edges by lining the inside with a bit of the cornstarch mixture. Place the dumpling on a lightly greased plate. Repeat with the remaining ingredients until used up, and steam the dumplings in a steaming basket lined with cabbage leaves for 3 minutes.
3 Combine the sweet black soy sauce with the balsamic vinegar, mix well and dribble over the steamed dumplings. Serve hot, garnished with romaine lettuce.

Makes 8 dumplings   Preparation time: 20 minutes   Cooking time: 3 minutes

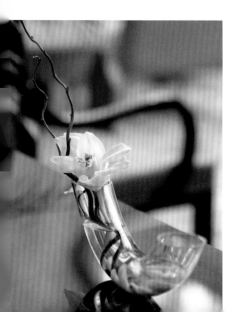

fruit cookie lollipops

This witty creation relies on two, easy-to-make biscuit mixtures, some lovely citrus flavors and just a beginners' skill with an icing bag, for full impact. Drawing the circle outlines on the greaseproof paper first will help in the forming of accurate circles.

Greaseproof baking paper
12 bamboo skewers

Fruit Filling
$^1/_3$ cup (50 g) flour
Pinch of salt
$^1/_3$ cup (80 ml) Thai orange (*som*) or calamansi juice
3 tablespoons (50 g) melted butter
$^1/_2$ cup (100 g) superfine castor sugar
$^1/_2$ teaspoon grated orange zest
$^1/_2$ teaspoon grated lemon zest

Cookie Batter
4 tablespoons (80 g) melted butter
$^1/_2$ cup (70 g) icing or powdered sugar
2 egg whites
$^1/_2$ cup (75 g) flour
1 drop vanilla essence

1 To make the Fruit Filling, sift the flour and salt together and set aside. Heat the juice in a saucepan over low heat until warm. Set aside. Whisk the butter and sugar in a bowl until light and fluffy, then fold in a little warm juice followed by a tablespoon of the salted flour, and mix well. Continue to add in this manner until all the juice and flour are incorporated, then stir in the orange and lemon zest. Set aside

2 To make the Cookie Batter, whisk the butter and icing or powdered sugar in a bowl until light and fluffy. Gradually fold in a little of the egg whites followed by 1 tablespoon of the flour and mix well. Continue to add in this manner until all the egg whites and flour are incorporated, then stir in the vanilla essence. Set aside.

3 Preheat the oven to 400°F (200°C).

4 To assemble, line a sheet pan with greaseproof baking paper. Transfer the Cookie Batter mixture into an icing bag and pipe out 12 circles that are each about 3 in (7 cm) in diameter onto the greaseproof paper. Lay a soaked bamboo skewer on each circle such that 1 in (2$^1/_2$ cm) of its tip is inside the circle, then top the center of each circle with $^1/_2$ tablespoon of the Fruit Filling mixture. Bake in the oven at 400°F (200°C) for 8 to 10 minutes.

Makes 12 sticks   Preparation time: 40 minutes   Cooking time: 10 minutes

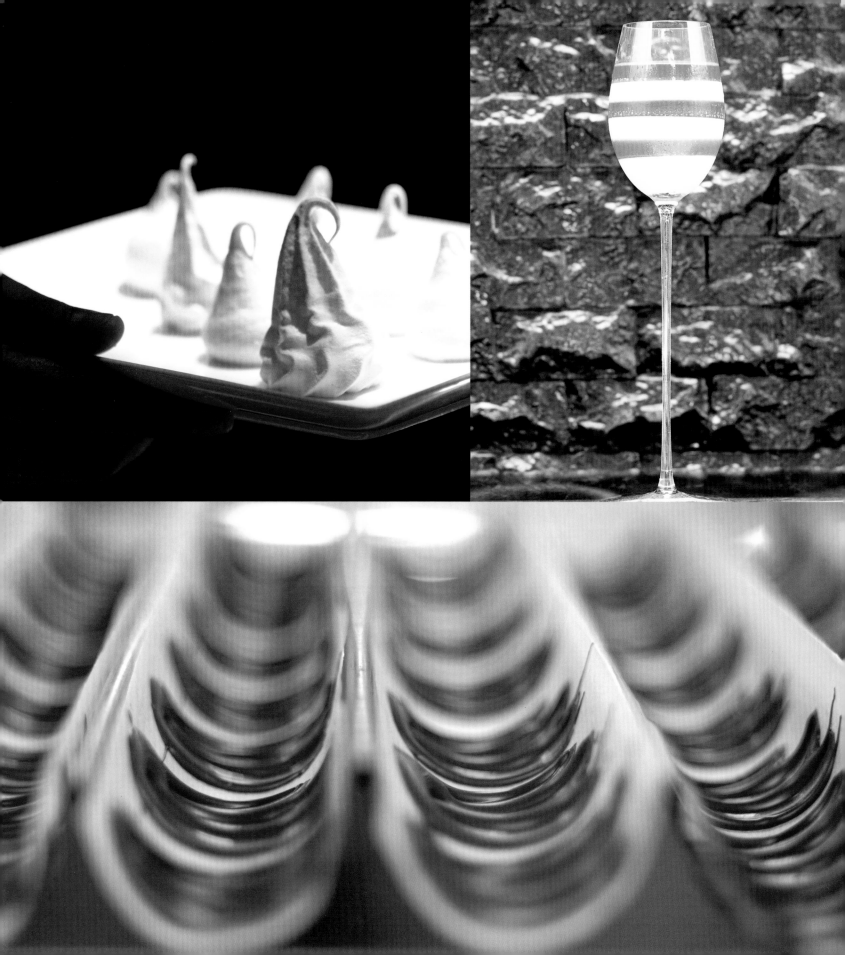

coconut pannacotta with lavender jelly, mangosteen meringue and melted chocolate

Pannacotta, which translates from the Italian as "cooked cream" has become very modish on restaurant menus over the past few years. With its chic simplicity, it lends itself to all manner of embellishments, such as the coconut and mangosteen flavors employed here.

4 fresh mangosteens or 1 can (1$^1/_4$ lbs/560 g) mangosteens in syrup

Lavender Jelly
4 cups (1 liter) water
$^1/_3$ cup (65 g) sugar
1$^1/_2$ tablespoons dried lavender flowers
12 gelatin leaves or 3 tablespoons gelatin powder
4 cups (1 liter) ice water

Coconut Pannacotta
$^1/_2$ vanilla pod, sliced lengthwise, seeds removed with a spoon, or 1 teaspoon vanilla essence
1 cup (250 ml) fresh milk
4 tablespoons sugar
3 gelatin leaves or 2 teaspoons gelatin powder
1$^1/_4$ cups (300 ml) thick coconut milk

Meringue
2 egg whites
$^2/_3$ cup (125 g) sugar
Pinch of salt

Melted Chocolate
4 bars (200 g) Chocolate couverture, finely chopped
Bain-Marie (lukewarm water bath)
Pinch of salt

1 To make the Lavender Jelly, bring the water and sugar to a boil in a saucepan over medium heat. Remove once the sugar has completely dissolved. Add the lavender flowers and set aside to infuse for 1 hour, then strain into a small saucepan. Soak the gelatin leaves in ice water for about 3 minutes to soften. In the meantime, heat the lavender infusion over low heat until hot. Remove and place the saucepan in the bowl of ice water, and gradually whisk in the softened gelatin leaves or gelatin powder. Set aside to cool to room temperature.

2 To make the Coconut Pannacotta, soak the gelatin leaves in ice water for about 3 minutes to soften. Bring the vanilla seeds, fresh milk and sugar to a boil in a saucepan, then whisk in the softened gelatin leaves or gelatin powder, followed by the coconut milk. Remove and set aside to cool to room temperature.

3 To assemble, fill $^1/_3$ of the serving glasses with the Coconut Pannacotta and chill in the refrigerator. Once the Pannacotta is firmed, top with the Lavender Jelly and chill again in the refrigerator.

4 To make the Meringue, preheat the oven to 160°F (80°C). Whisk the egg whites and salt at high speed in a mixer and gradually add in the sugar until stiff. Transfer the mixture to a piping bag and pipe small mounds onto a lightly greased baking sheet. Bake in the oven at 160°F (80°C) for 1$^1/_2$ hours.

5 To make the Melted Chocolate, place the Chocolate couverture in a stainless steel bowl and place the bowl on top of the Bain-Marie, stirring occasionally, until the chocolate melts completely, Transfer to a serving bowl and serve immediately.

6 Top the Coconut Pannacotta and Lavender Jelly with 2 segments of mangosteen and serve chilled with the Meringue and Melted Chocolate.

Note: Take great care not to drip any water into the chocolate to avoid coagulation and do not overheat or the chocolate will crystallize.

Makes 6 to 8 servings   Preparation time: 1 hour   Cooking time: 2 hours

tea muffins

Perfumed spices like cardamom, cloves and cinnamon serve to intensify the flavor of coffee, for which elegant little muffins like these are the absolutely perfect foil.

5 oz (150 g) butter

$1^1/_4$ cups (250 g) sugar

3 eggs

$2^3/_4$ cups (400 g) flour

$1^1/_2$ tablespoons baking powder

1 teaspoon vanilla

1 teaspoon salt

$^3/_4$ cup (200 ml) milk

1 tablespoon green tea

3 tablespoons rose bud tea

5 tablespoons jasmine tea

$^1/_3$ cup coarsely chopped water chest-nuts (80 g, about 4 water chestnuts)

$^1/_2$ cup (80 g) bittersweet chocolate chips

$^1/_2$ cup (80 g) fresh ripe mango cubes

1 Preheat the oven to 425°F (210°C).

2 Beat the butter and sugar with a mixer or wooden spoon until the sugar dissolves. Add the eggs and continue to beat until light and foamy. Stir in the flour, baking powder, vanilla and salt. Mix well and divide the batter into 3 equal portions. Set aside.

3 Combine $^1/_4$ cup (50 ml) of the milk and the green tea in a saucepan, mix well and simmer over medium heat for about 1 minute, until the tea flavor is absorbed. Strain and discard the tea leaves, reserving the liquid. Do the same with $^1/_4$ cup (50 ml) of the milk and the rosebud tea, and finally $^1/_2$ cup (100 ml) of the milk and the jasmine tea, adding each portion of the milk tea to one portion of the batter and blending well.

4 Add the water chestnuts to the green tea batter, the chocolate chips to the rosebud batter and the mango cubes to the jasmine tea batter. Mix each batter well and transfer to small muffin molds, making sure to fill each mold up to only $^3/_4$ full.

5 Place the muffins in the oven and bake for 20 minutes. Serve warm with Spiced Sumatran Coffee.

Makes 10 to 12   Preparation time: 60 minutes   Cooking time: 20 minutes

spiced sumatran coffee (café brûlot)

2 tablespoons sugar

4 cups brewed coffee

1 orange

3 cloves

1 cinnamon stick

3 cardamom pods

1 jigger dark rum

1 Heat the sugar in a saucepan over low heat, then squeeze the juice of the orange over it and continue to heat until caramelized, about 5 minutes. Add the cloves, cinnamon and cardamoms and mix well, then add the rum and flambé the mixture. Pour in the coffee and simmer over low heat for about 5 minutes until the caramel is completely blended with the coffee.

2 Pour into 8 cups and serve with Tea Muffins.

Makes 8 small espresso cups   Preparation time: 15 minutes
Cooking time: 10 minutes

tropical tiramisu

Sago, derived from a variety of palm trees, often forms the basis for many desserts in Asia. Here it contributes to a playful departure from the traditional tiramisu—where tropical fruits, instead of the expected chocolate and espresso, give oomph to a creamy mascarpone base.

2 passion fruits (see note), cracked open, flesh scooped into a bowl
3 tablespoons (80 g) pomelo or grape-fruit pulp
3$^1/_2$ tablespoons dried sago pearls
4 halved Lady's Finger biscuits or 8 thin slices of sponge cake

Tiramisu
1 cup (4 oz /125 g) mascarpone cheese
$^1/_2$ cup (125 g) cream
3 tablespoons sugar
1 egg

1 To make the Tiramisu, whisk all the ingredients with a mixer at high speed for about 15 minutes until stiff. Set aside.
2 Combine the passion fruit and pomelo pulp in a bowl and mix well. Set aside.
3 Cover the sago pearls with water in a saucepan and boil for about 30 minutes until the pearls are translucent. Remove and rinse under running water. Drain and set aside.
4 To assemble, reserve 1 tablespoon of the fruit mixture and divide the rest into 8 portions. Place each portion and a piece of Lady's Finger biscuit or a slice of sponge cake in a small serving bowl, and top with the Tiramisu in the center, then the sago on the side, all around the Tiramisu. Finally place a small amount of the reserved fruit mixture on top of the Tiramisu. Repeat with all the other passion fruit pomelo portions in this manner and serve chilled.

Note: If passion fruit is not available, try using ripe fresh mango or papaya, peeled and diced. Dried sago pearls are sold in boxes and plastic packets in Asian food stores. They are tiny, white pearls that become translucent when boiled.

Makes 8 portions   Preparation time: 45 minutes   Cooking time: 30 minutes

ingredients

Agar-agar is a gelatin made from freeze-drying and dehydrating the fronds of a combination of red algae. It is used as a thickening agent in soups, sauces and desserts. Available in the form of bars, strips, flakes and powder, agar-agar can be purchased from the dry food section of many supermarkets. Powdered agar-agar can be substituted in equal measure for powdered plain gelatin, but do not mix it with vinegar or foods high in oxalic acid like spinach or chocolate as it will not set.

Bamboo shoots are the young sprouting stems of the bamboo plant. Fresh cream colored shoots can be purchased at Asian stores. Boil them until tender, remove the green outer leaves and only use the tender shoot inside. Also available are canned and vacuum packed precooked bamboo shoot which can be bought in most supermarkets. Rinse well before using. To store, soak in a bowl of fresh water in the refrigerator, changing water daily, for up to 10 days.

Banana leaf is indispensable as a food wrapper, used to wrap food for steaming or grilling, as little trays to hold food for steaming and used as a kind of cookie cup for sweetness. The moisture within the banana leaf makes a difference to the texture and flavor of the food, but if you cannot find fresh or frozen banana leaf, replace with aluminium foil.

Bean curd or tofu, is a soft food made from curdling fresh soybean milk with a coagulant. Three main types of bean curd are available in most grocery stores: **Firm bean curd** (*tau kwa* or *tou gan*) has been compressed to expel most of the moisture and forms a dense and solid cake. It is normally deep-fried and holds up well in stir-fried dishes or on the grill. **Soft bean curd** is reasonably soft and sold in blocks, immersed in water. It is generally used in soups and braised dishes and makes a good choice for recipes that call for blended bean curd. **Silken bean curd** is very soft. It is best steamed or added to soups. Sold in plastic rolls, it does not stir-fry well and tends to crumble. Fresh bean curd has a very short shelf life. Refrigerate immersed in water.

Black bean sauce is a dark sauce made from fermented black soybeans and available in various consistencies. It may be thick and contain chunks of fermented black soybeans or smooth and thin. A variation is hot black bean sauce, which has chili paste added, and black bean garlic sauce. With a full flavored and salty taste, it is a common seasoning for fish and beef. Sold in small jars in Asian food stores, black bean sauce can be stored for months refrigerated. Use brown bean sauce if not available.

Black Chinese vinegar or *hei chu*, is a dark, almost smoky flavored vinegar made from glutinous or sweet rice, although millet and sorghum may be used instead. Often used in Chinese dishes, black Chinese vinegar works well in braised dishes and as a dipping sauce. Bottled black Chinese vinegar is available from supermarkets and Asian food stores. Balsamic or rice vinegar can be used as a substitute.

Bok choy, also known as *pak choy* or Chinese chard, is a crunchy juicy cabbage used widely in Chinese stir-fried dishes. A small vegetable with plump white stalks and dark green leaves, fresh bok choy is available year-round in supermarkets and Asian markets. Look for bok choy with thick fleshy firm stalks and unblemished green leaves. For storage, refrigerate in a loosely closed plastic bag for no more than 2 days.

Bonito flakes are shavings from dried tuna fish. Having a strong, salty flavor and a tan color, bonito flakes are frequently sprinkled over boiled or steamed vegetables and soups to add flavor. Packets of bonito flakes can be bought from Japanese supermarkets.

Caraway seeds are aromatic seeds of a herb in the parsley family. With a nutty, peppery aroma and delicate anise flavor, they are used widely in German, Austrian and Hungarian cuisines for flavoring cheese, bread, cakes, stew, meat and vegetable. Caraway seeds are used whole, added to or sprinkled over food. Store airtight in a cool place for no more than 6 months.

Cardamom is a pungent spice commonly used in Indian cuisine. Pale green, straw-colored or black, the cardamom pods enclose about 15 to 20 intensely fragrant brown or black cardamom seeds. Cardamom is used to perfume rice dishes, curries, cakes and desserts. Available as powder, seeds or whole pods in most Asian food stores, the best flavor is achieved by using the seeds removed from the pod directly.

Ready-ground cardamom is not recommended as it loses its fragrance very quickly.

Caul fat is the lacy thin membrane that lines the belly of pigs or lambs. It is often used as a wrapper for sausage. Not widely available, you may need to order it from your butcher. Soak caul fat in milk or vinegar and water to get rid of any ammonia taste before using.

Caviar is fresh sturgeon roe known for its subtle and buttery flavor. Due to over-fishing, caviar is no longer readily available and is very highly priced. Replace with the French farmed varieties or the cheaper black lumpfish roe. Perk up an inferior caviar with a splash of fresh lemon juice.

Chervil, also known as *cicily*, is an aromatic herb with curly, dark green leaves that has a slight aniseed fragrance. A member of the parsley family, it is used like parsley but its delicate flavor is diminished when boiled. Also available dried, it has the best fragrance and flavor when fresh.

Chickpea flour, also known as garbanzo flour, is milled from dried and ground chickpeas and is commonly used in Mediterranean cuisine. A good substitute is *besan* or *channa* flour, which is milled from yellow split peas (*channa dal*). Both flour are similar in color and texture and can be found in health food and Indian grocery stores.

Chinese cabbage that is most popular and often seen in the supermarkets is the napa cabbage. The plant forms a head with leaves and petioles when matured. A common ingredient in Asian stir-fries, this vegetable is very tender and delicious. Fresh Chinese cabbage is available year round in most supermarkets.

Chinese rice wine is used in Asian cooking in much the same way as sherry or white wine is used in Western cooking. Bottled rice wine is obtainable from supermarkets and Asian food stores. Use sake or dry sherry as a substitute.

Chinese sausage or *lap cheong*, is the dried, rather hard and chewy Chinese sausage made from pork. It is smoked, sweet and highly seasoned. Perfumed with rose-flavored wine, it is never eaten alone, but cooked with rice or other food. Chinese sausages are sold in Chinese grocery shops and can be seen tied and hanging in bunches or in netting bags. They are finger-sized and bright red in color. Chinese sausage keeps well in a dry place and can be stored refrigerated up to several months. Briefly soak in water and remove the gelatin skin before using. Use sweet dried salami as a substitute.

Coriander is a pungent herb essential to many Southeast Asian cuisines. The whole plant is used. The seeds are the most popular spice. For maximum freshness, whole seeds are dry-roasted and ground before used. **Coriander leaves**, also known as cilantro or Chinese parsley, have a distinctive smell and attractive appearance and are used for their fresh flavor and as a garnish. Coriander root is a popular Thai seasoning. For storage, wash and dry the fresh leaves and refrigerate, wrapped in a plastic bag.

Cumin seeds are similar in appearance to caraway seeds. Dark brown and ridged on the outside, the seeds are often roasted and ground before using. The earthy aroma is distinct, its flavor often likened to liquorice.

Curry leaves are leaves from the curry leaf tree, and belong to the same family as lemon. They do not taste like curry, but are named for their frequent use in Indian curries. Curry leaves are generally sold in sprigs consisting of 12 to 16 small, slightly pointed dull green leaves. Fresh or dried curry leaves are available. Dried curry leaves are milder, but are a more satisfactory substitute than *salam* or bay leaves. There is no substitute for curry leaves.

Curry powder is a spice blend made from various combinations of ground spices that generally include cumin, coriander seeds, chilies, turmeric, ginger, cinnamon and cloves. Different spice combinations vary in color and flavor. Look for curry powder in well stocked supermarkets.

Daikon, also known as Japanese radish or Mooli, is a giant white radish with a sweet and fresh flavor. Its crispy and juicy white flesh is often used raw in Asian salads and cooking. Choose those that are firm and unwrinkled. Daikon can be stored for up to 2 weeks, wrapped in a plastic bag and refrigerated.

Dashi is a basic Japanese soup stock used extensively in Japanese cooking. It is made from dried bonito flakes or dried kelp and water. You can purchase *dashi* in bottles or as instant stock powder from Japanese supermarkets, which is then simply added to boiling water. *Dashi* stock may be stored in a sealed bottle in the refrigerator for up to 3 days.

Dried shrimp paste, also known as *belachan* or *trasi*, is a dense mixture of fermented group shrimp with a remarkably strong odor. Widely used to flavor Asian cuisine, dried shrimp paste is sold in dried blocks in Asian food stores and ranges in color from pink to blackish-brown. It should be slightly roasted to enhance its flavor before using.

Fennel is an aromatic vegetable with pale green, celery-like stems and bright green, feathery foliage. Both the base and stems can be eaten raw in salads or cooked by braising or sautèing, or added to soups. This fragrant greenery is also used as a garnish or snipped for

a last-minute flavor enhancer. Choose clean, crisp bulbs with no sign of browning and fresh green leaves. Refrigerate wrapped in a plastic bag up to 5 days.

Filo pastry or filo dough are fragile, paper-thin sheets of dough that are usually basted with melted butter and then stacked until they are many layers thick. The dough dries out quickly, so always cover any unused dough with plastic wrap or a damp cloth. Both fresh and frozen filo pastry are sold in supermarkets. Fresh pastry is preferred as it doesn't tear easily. Defrost frozen filo pastry before using. If not available, puff pastry dough can be used as a substitute.

Fish sauce, known as *nam pla* in Thailand and *nuoc nom* in Vietnam, is made from salted, fermented fish or shrimp. Sold in bottles, good quality fish sauce is clear and golden-brown, and has a salty tang. The Vietnamese variety is more intense in flavor and darker in color than the Thai variety. As Thai fish sauce is quite salty, use sparingly. Fish sauce keeps indefinitely in a cupboard.

Five spice powder is a blend of fragrant sweet spices including cinnamon, star anise, cloves, fennel seeds and Sichuan pepper. This reddish-brown powder is popular as a seasoning in Chinese cuisine and some Thai and Vietnamese dishes. Pre-packaged five spice powder is avail-

able in Asian markets and well stocked supermarkets. To keep its freshness as long as possible, store it in the refrigerator.

Foie gras, a French delicacy, is simply the goose or duck liver that has been lightly cooked. When aged, it becomes very rich and flavorful. Goose liver is tastier and more expensive than duck liver. Some refuse to eat foie gras because the animals are force-fed to enlarge their livers. Available flash frozen, whole or sliced.

Galangal is a rhizome belonging to the ginger family. Known as *kha* in Thailand, *laos* in Indonesia and *lengkuas* in Malaysia and Singapore, it adds a distinctive fragrance and flavor to many curry dishes. Though available as a powder, most food stores sell fresh root for its richer flavor. Fresh root should be peeled before using. Will keep for several months if stored in an airtight container in the freezer.

Hoisin sauce or Peking sauce, is a sweet and spicy reddish-brown sauce made from soybeans, garlic, peppers and various spices. Commonly usied as a table condiment and flavoring agent for meat, poultry and shellfish dishes, this Chinese sauce can be sourced from many supermarkets. Canned *hoisin* should be stored refrigerated in a non-metal airtight container. Bottled *hoisin* will keep indefinitely when refrigerated.

Kadaifa or *katafi*, is a form of filo dough used by Middle Eastern cooks to make sweet desserts. These long, thin strands of pastry are sold fresh or frozen in specialty markets. The packaged form of *kadaifa* looks very much like rice vermicelli or coils of very thin dried pasta. Always keep it from drying as you work with it. Cover any unused dough with a damp cloth. You may use filo pastry cut into very thin strands as a substitute.

Kailan, also known as *gai lan*, Chinese broccoli or Chinese kale, is a crunchy vegetable with small slender dark to mid-green stalks, lots of very dark green leaves and white flowers. The entire vegetable can be boiled, steamed and stir-fried. Choose heads with full, dark green leaves and fresh stalks. Refrigerate, unwashed in a plastic bag for no more than 2 to 3 days.

Kangkong is a popular and highly nutritious leafy green vegetable also known as morning glory, water convolvulus or water spinach. It has long hollow stems with pointed, mid-green leaves, which have a soft and crunchy texture and appealing mild flavor when cooked. Young shoots may be eaten raw as salad or with a dip. The leaves and tender stems are usually braised. Fresh *kangkong* is widely available now in supermarkets or Asian food stores. *Kangkong* does not keep well; wrap in newspaper or cloth and refrigerate for 1 to 2 days. If not available, use spinach or bok choy as a substitute.

Kimchi is a salted and spicy fermented Korean pickle, usually made with Chinese cabbage or turnips and seasoned with liberal amounts of chili and garlic. Served as a side dish as well as an ingredient in stir-fries and soups. Kimchi can be purchased vacuum-packed or bottled in Korean markets and well stocked supermarkets, and keeps indefinitely refrigerated.

Konbu, also known as *kombu* or kelp, is a type of dried seaweed used primarily as a flavoring in *dashi*, though it may also be deep-fried or stir-fried. It is usually sold dried, in strips or sheets and keeps indefinitely if refrigerated in a tightly sealed container. Choose *Konbu* that is very dark. Wipe with a dry cloth but do not wash before using.

Lemongrass is a lemon-scented stalk which grows in clumps and is very important in Southeast Asia cuisine. Remove and discard the dry outer leaves and use the pale, white part of the stem (the bottom 3 in/8 cm). Available fresh, frozen or dried, fresh lemongrass is preferred for its stronger smell and flavor.

Mace is the red outer lacy covering of the nutmeg seed, hence it tastes and smells like a pungent nutmeg. Dried mace is yellow-orange and sold ground and less frequently, whole (in "blades"). Having a fragrant, sweet and delicious flavor, mace is a spice used to flavor all sorts of foods, from sweet to savory.

Mirin is a very sweet sake made by mixing and fermenting steamed glutinous rice with *shoju*, a distilled spirit similar to vodka. It adds a lovely glaze to grilled foods and a mild sweetness in cooking. Bottled *mirin* is available in well stocked supermarkets and Japanese supermarkets. If not available, use sake added with sugar or dry sherry added with sugar as a substitute.

Miso paste is a Japanese fermented soybean paste made from cultivating soybeans in either a barley, rice or soybean base. It comes in a variety of flavors and colors, such as white, beige, red and brown. The lighter-colored miso such as the **white miso** is the sweet variety and usually used in soups, sauces and for marinating fish. The darker-colored miso is salty and normally used in heavier dishes. Sold in plastic containers, miso can be sourced from well stocked supermarkets.

Nori is a type of seaweed pressed into very thin sheets and baked or seasoned with sweetened soy sauce. It is sold in large and medium sheets and usually packed in stacks of 10. **Nori flakes** are the flakes of *nori* sheets, often added to Japanese dishes for flavoring. It can be purchased in plastic packets in Asian grocery stores and Japanese supermarkets.

Pandanus leaves, also known as pandan leaves or screwpine leaves, are long thin leaves used to impart a delicate fragrance and sweet, grassy flavor into rice, cakes and desserts. They are also used as wrappers for seasoned morsels, cakes and desserts. Though they can be deep-frozen, always look for fresh leaves at the supermarkets or Asian markets. A few drops of bottled pandan or vanilla essence is a good substitute.

Pimento is a large, heart-shaped sweet pepper that is sweeter, more succulent and aromatic than the normal red bell pepper. Fresh pimento is rare, but canned and bottled grilled pimentos are available all year-round in specialty markets and well stocked supermarkets.

Pomelo is a citrus fruit similar to a grapefruit, but larger in size and with a pointed stem. Smooth green in colour, its pulp is milder and sweeter. Pomelo is sold fresh in Asian food stores. Use grapefruit added with a bit of sugar as a substitute.

Ponzu is a mixture of lemon juice or rice vinegar, soy sauce, *mirin*, sake, *konbu* and dried bonito flakes. It is often used as a Japanese dipping sauce with dishes like sashimi. Sold in small bottles, *ponzu* is available in well stocked supermarkets and Japanese supermarkets.

Potato flour is a fine white gluten-free flour made from cooked, dried and ground potatoes. It is often used as a thickener, especially in baked food as it produces a moist crumb. It is mixed with wheat flour to make **potato starch**.

Radicchio is a bitter and peppery Italian chicory often used as a salad green. Different varieties with leaves ranging from deep red to white in color are available. Choose heads that have crisp, full-colored leaves with no sign of browning. Store in a plastic bag in the refrigerator for up to a week.

Rice paper wrappers are dried, white, textured sheets made from rice flour and available in round or square sheets. They are brittle, so soak briefly in warm water to soften before using. Pat dry with paper towels to absorb any excess water. Sold in Asian food stores, they will keep for many months if stored in a cool, dark place.

Rice vermicelli, also known as *beehoon* or *mifen*, are very fine dried noodle threads made from rice flour. They are used throughout Asia in soups, spring rolls, cold salads and stir-fries. Packets of dried rice vermicelli are widely available in supermarkets. Soak dried rice vermicelli in water until softened and drain before using.

Saffron is a pungent, aromatic spice used primarily to flavor and tint food. It is the world's most expensive spice obtained by carefully hand-picking and drying the stamen, or hair-like stalks, of the saffron crocus. Available in both powdered form and threads in Asian food stores, powdered saffron loses its flavor more readily. The threads should be crushed just before using. Store airtight in a cool, dark place for up to 6 months.

Sake or Japanese rice wine, is the national alcoholic drink of Japan made from fermented rice. The yellowish slightly sweet sake is used in Japanese cooking, particularly in sauces and marinades. It should be consumed within a year of bottling. Once opened, keep it tightly sealed in the refrigerator up to 3 weeks. Use Chinese rice wine or dry sherry as a substitute.

Sambal oelek is an Indonesian chili paste containing ground red chili, garlic, shallots, candlenuts, galangal, turmeric, palm sugar and kaffir lime leaves. Used in cooking or as an accompaniment, this chili paste is available in jars and bottles from supermarkets and Asian stores.

Sancho pepper is a powder made from the ground leaves of the prickly ash plant. It has a peppery flavor with a slight lemon tang, which is quite similar to Sichuan pepper. Small bottles of *sancho* pepper are obtainable in specialty markets and well stocked supermarkets. If not available, Sichuan pepper may be used as a substitute.

Sesame oil is pressed from sesame seeds. The lighter-colored sesame oil has a deliciously nutty nuance and is used for everything from salad dressing to sautèing. Korean and Japanese sesame oil is lighter and milder than the darker Asian variety and is used to flavor as well as to season. As sesame oil can be quite strong, use sparingly. Bottled sesame oil is readily available in many supermarkets.

Sesame paste is the nutty cream brown paste made from ground toasted sesame seeds. It is sold in cans or jars in well stocked supermarkets and keeps indefinitely after opening. A suitable substitute is peanut butter added with sesame oil.

Sherry vinegar, also known as Xérès, is the Spanish vinegar that is assertive yet smooth and great for perking up sauces, especially those that accompany hearty meats such as duck or beef. If not available, use Balsamic vinegar or red wine vinegar instead.

Shiitake mushrooms are dark brown with a smooth velvety cap. They are large and meaty and work well in stir-fries, soups and side dishes. Dried shiitakes are more commonly known as black Chinese mushrooms and are suitable for dishes that require intense flavor. Shiitake mushrooms are available fresh or dried and packaged whole, sliced, in pieces or crumbs, in a variety of sizes. Soak them in hot water for about 15 minutes to reconstitute, then use the water they soaked in to enhance your sauce.

Soba noodles are chewy Japanese noodles made with a blend of wheat and buckwheat flour. They are often sold fresh in Japan but are only available dried overseas. Soba noodles come in different widths and flavors, including green tea (*chasoba*) and yam (*yamaimo*). They are sold in Japanese supermarkets in packets and look like short linguine. Blanch dried soba for about 5 to 7 minutes to soften before using. Udon or spaghetti makes a good substitute.

Soy sauce is made from fermented soybeans that have been salted. It is used throughout Asia with different regions producing quite different varieties. Japanese soy sauce, known as *shoyu*, comes in light and black varieties. Normal soy sauce, commonly used as a table dip and seasoning, is the saltiest, while dark soy sauce contributes color and flavor. Use top quality

or top grade soy sauce as it is less salty than the other grades.

Spanish chorizo is a spicy Spanish sausage made from beef and/or pork. Unlike the Mexican chorizo which needs to be cooked, Spanish chorizo is dry-cured and ready to eat. Pepperoni or any dry-cured pork sausage makes a good substitute.

Star anise, or badiane, is a dried brown flower with eight woody petals. Each of these petals contains a seed. It has a strong aniseed and cinnamon flavor and aroma. Asian cooks use star anise to give a liquorice flavor to savory dishes, particularly those with pork and poultry. It is available whole or ground. If used whole, discard before serving.

Sukiyaki beef is sold in Japanese supermarkets overseas—it is very high-quality beef that has been shaved into ultra-thin strips. If you cannot find it, buy a thick, well marbled steak and put it in the freezer wrapped in plastic wrap for about 1 hour until half frozen. Unwrap the steak and using a very sharp knife, shave the steak lengthwise to obtain long, narrow strips about 6 x 1$\frac{1}{2}$ in (15 x 4 cm) and $\frac{1}{8}$ in (3 mm) thick.

Tandoori spice powder is a hot blend of spice used in Indian cuisine, usually includes chili, *garam masala*, turmeric and saffron. It can be purchased ready-made from Asian groceries and well stocked supermarkets.

Tapioca flour (*tam min fun*) is also known as cassava flour. Top quality tapioca flour is used to make *dim sum* dough. It has the capacity to absorb a lot of water and steam and gives the dough excellent elasticity. Purchase packets that are labelled as extra fine, grade 1 or grade A flour. It is also used as a thickening agent.

Thai basil (*horapa*) is a fragrant tropical herb easily recognizable by its purple stem, green leaves and exquisite aniseed flavor. It is liberally used to perfume and augment food in Thai cuisine—a favorite in Thai stir-fries and curries or as a garnish. Thai basil can lose its fragrance very quickly, so it is best to buy them on the day of use. As refrigeration can ruin its flavor, store Thai basil upright in a little water, covered.

Thyme is a pungent minty and lemony herb widely used to flavor stew and sauces, and often used with other herbs like rosemary, parsley and oregano. Fresh thyme is far more flavorful than the dried thyme, and is obtainable from supermarkets during the summer months.

Dried thyme is available year-round in leaf and powder form.

Turmeric is a member of the ginger family. This orange-yellow rhizome has a very rich yellow interior and a pleasant pungency. Available as a fresh root or powder, it is used mainly to color food. The fresh root must be peeled, then grated or sliced before using.

Vietnamese mint, also known as *daun kesum*, *laksa* leaves or Cambodian mint leaves, are not true mint leaves despite having a minty flavor. This peppery flavored herb is used in Singapore, Malaysia and Vietnam in laksa soups. Laksa leaves are sold fresh in bunches in Asian grocery stores and should always be used fresh. Asian or sweet basil can be used as a substitute.

Wakame is the long, narrow, ribbon-like strands, dark green Japanese seaweed. Both fresh and dried are available in specialty markets and Japanese supermarkets. Dried wakame should be stored in an airtight container in a dark, dry place. Soak dried wakame in plenty of water for 20 to 30 minutes, then briefly blanch in boiling water before using.

Wasabi or Japanese horseradish is the bright green condiment traditionally served with sushi, sashimi and noodle dishes in Japan. It has a sharp, pungent and fiery flavor. Available in both paste and powder forms in

specialty and Asian markets, wasabi is prepared by grating the fresh rhizome of the wasabi plant.

Water chestnut is a tuber that resembles a chestnut in color and shape. Available fresh, processed and canned, this firm and crispy textured Chinese vegetable is easily sourced in supermarkets and Asian stores. Fresh water chestnuts can be stored refrigerated up to a week, soaking in water.

Wagyu beef is the highly evenly marbled beef from cattle of the *Wagyu* breed, renowned for its melt-in-the-mouth tenderness, succulent texture and tastiest flavor. *Wagyu* beef from the *Wagyu* cattle raised in Kobe, Japan is known as *kobe* beef. Once only sold in Japan, it is now available in America and Australia, but is very expensive due to the specialized treatment in raising the cattle—pampered cattle are massaged with sake and fed a special diet that includes plenty of beer. Any thinly sliced loin beef with marbled fat can be used as a substitute.

Wonton wrappers or wonton skins are square or round uncooked wrappers made of flour, eggs and water. Available in different sizes and thickness, they are used with a wide variety of fillings. The thin ones work best in soups, while the thicker ones are best for frying. Available frozen or fresh, look for stacks of them wrapped in plastic in Asian markets. Store

them chilled but thaw to room temperature before using.

XO sauce is a Hong Kong delicacy made of dried shredded scallops and shrimp cooked with fragrant spices and oil. A luxurious item named after the extra old premium cognac, it is similar to its namesake in that it keeps well and tastes even better with age. Now widely available bottled in Asian food stores, for a substitute, fry chili oil with chopped dried shrimp, chili, garlic, shallots, sugar and salt, and cook over low heat for 45 minutes.

Yuzu is a zesty Japanese citrus fruit used for its aromatic rind that is milder than lemons and limes but not bitter. *Yuzu* is used as a garnish or added to dishes to enhance their flavor. Lemon juice sweetened with a sprinkling of sugar is a good substitute.

Zucchini blossoms are very popular in Italian cooking, but not widely available. Look for them at the local farmers' markets or boutique produce stores. They have a very short shelf life, so be sure to buy them only on the day of use. Flowers from any squash are good substitutes.

acknowledgments

The publisher and authors would like to thank Octavio Gamarra and the management and staff of The Ritz-Carlton, Millenia Singapore for their assistance and support in the creation of this book, in particular project managers Evelyn Yo and Gilles Perrin, and the following individuals: (from left to right in photos above) Chinese Chef de Cuisine Fok Kai Yee (left) and team, Pastry Chef Philippe Agnese with Assistant Pastry Chef Jong Tze Khang (left) and Executive Baker Michael Lim Chon Ping (right), Chef de Cuisine Gilles Perrin and Assistant Public Relations Manager Evelyn Yo, Chef de Cuisine Benton Toh with Butcher Chef Wong Hua Swan (left) and Junior Sous Chef Toh Li Liang (right), Chef de Cuisine Jason Ong and Sous Chef Vincent Kuek, Executive Steward Colin Lim and Assistant Lee Ker Shiun, Chinese Banquet Chef Raymond Yam and Junior Sous Chef Sam Choon Mun, Indian Chef Sharma Nand, Chef de Cuisine Jeffrey Tan and team, Culinary Administrative Assistant Leong Soke Yin and Assistant Director of Food and Beverage Roy Goh.

We would also like to thank Chia Meow Huay, Christina Ong, Magdalene Ong, Amos Lim, Cynthia Ho, Jasper Lee, Jordan Chong, Koh Chee Meng, Lee Ker Shiun, Russ Jaafar, Seah Geok Tin, Tan Gim Thye, Edmond Ho and Allan Tan.

A special thanks to the following retailers for the loan of their beautiful tableware: **CC Lee Marketing and Service**, 24 Verdun Road, Singapore 207282, T: (65) 6294-7975—**p.19** glass, **p.50** boxes; **p.69** bowl, **p.86** glasses; **p.119** bowl; **p.134** placemat; **DAUM,** 290 Orchard Road, #01-16 The Paragon, Singapore 238859, T: (65)6737-1454—**p.6** and **p.88**, **The Link Home**, #01-10, Palais Renaissance, 390 Orchard Road, Singapore 238871, T: (65)6737-7503—**p.28** placemats; **p.49** placemats; **p.57** glasses; **p.61** plates and forks, **p.74** placemat; **p.99** chopsticks; **Lotus Arts de Vivre**, #01-28, 328 North Bridge Road, The Raffles Hotel Arcade, Singapore 188719, T: (65)6334-2085—**p.117** bowl and spoon; **Phoebe Lentini Design,** Studio 17A, Carfield Commercial Building, 75-77 Wyndam Street, Central, Hong Kong, T: (852)3113-8003—**p.13** cocktail picks; **p.34** chopsticks; **p.39** plate

photo credits: p.7 by Vanessa Von Zitzewitz; **p.10** second right by Peter Mealin; **12** third right by Ho Yoke Weng; **23** by Edward Buay

art credits: 21 "Celia Birtwell" by David Hockney; **29** "Double Screw" by John Rose; **54** "Cornucopia" by Frank Stella; **p.81** by David Hockney; **96** by Rainer Gross.

stylist's own—**p.9**; **p.10**; **p.17**; **p.20**; **p.23**; **p.28**; **p.33**; **p.37**; **p.41**; **p.45**; **p.28**; **p.53**; **p.55**; **p.57**; **p.58**; **p.64**; **p.67**; **p.74**; **p.77**; **p.82**; **p.91**; **p.92**; **p.97**; **p.101**; **p.107**; **p.109**; **p.111**; **p.127**; **p.130**; **p.137**; **p.140**; **p.142**; **p.152**; **p.156**

Author's website: www.christophemegel.com

Published by Periplus Editions, with editorial offices at 130 Joo Seng Road #06-01, Singapore 368357

Copyright © 2004 Periplus Editions (HK) Ltd.
All rights reserved.
ISBN: 0-7946-0314-9

Distributors:

North America, Latin America, and Europe
Tuttle Publishing, 364 Innovation Drive, North Clarendon, VT 05759-9436, USA
Tel (802) 773 8930; fax (802) 773 6993 email: info@tuttlepublishing.com
www.tuttlepublishing.com

Japan Tuttle Publishing
Yaekari Building, 3F, 5-4-12 Osaki, Shinagawa-Ku, Tokyo 141 0032, Japan
Tel (813) 5437 0171; fax (813) 5437 0755 email: tuttle-sales@gol.com

Asia Pacific Berkeley Books Pte Ltd
130 Joo Seng Road #06-01, Singapore 368357 Tel (65) 6280 1330;
fax (65) 6280 6290 email: inquiries@periplus.com.sg www.periplus.com

Concept and direction by Christina Ong Book design by The Periplus Design Team

Index